Wallkill Valley Farmers' Association

The Wallkill Valley in art and story

Wallkill Valley Farmers' Association

The Wallkill Valley in art and story

ISBN/EAN: 9783337043094

Printed in Europe, USA, Canada, Australia, Japan

Cover: Foto ©ninafisch / pixelio.de

More available books at **www.hansebooks.com**

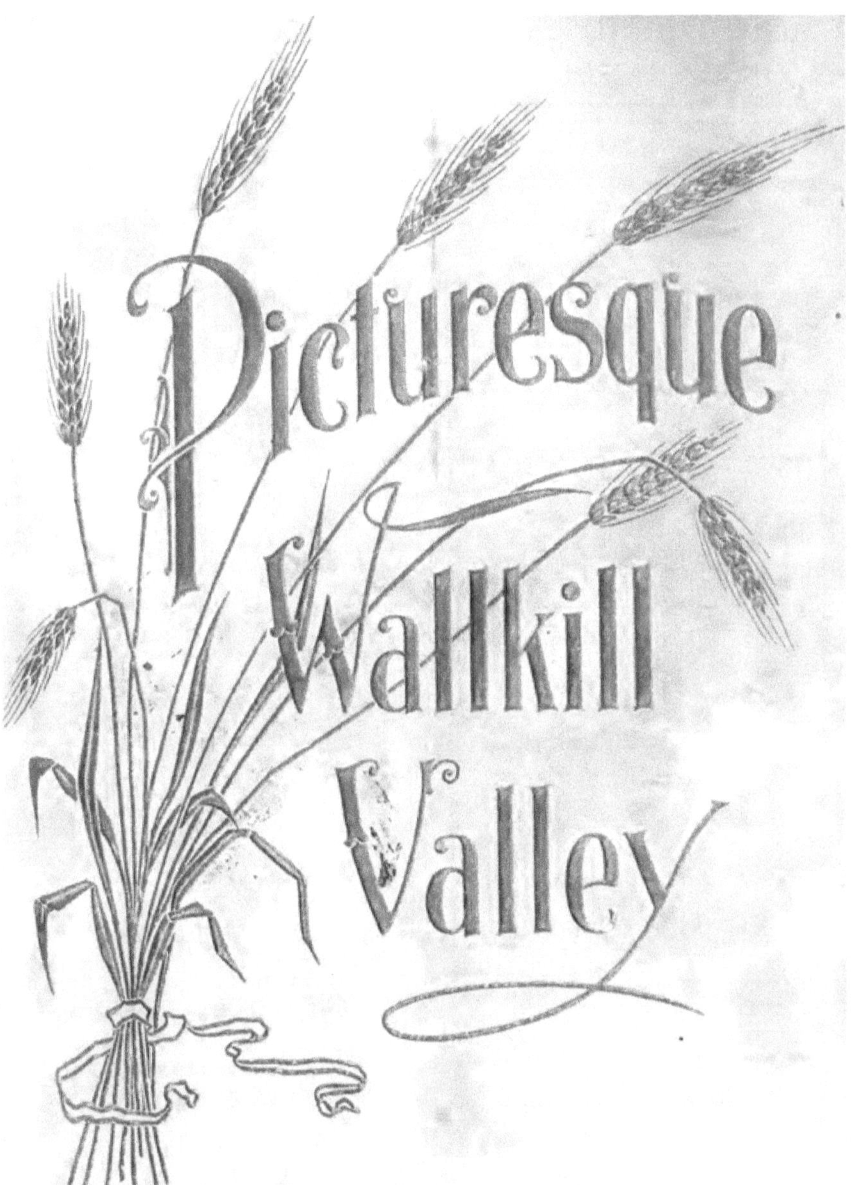
Picturesque
Wallkill
Valley

The Wallkill Valley

In Art and Story.

Its People
Its River
Its Environs
and
Its History

PUBLISHED BY

The Wallkill
Valley Farmers'
Association,
Walden, N. Y.

PRESS OF
JOHNSTON & PECK,
NEWBURGH, N. Y.

UNDER THE SUPERVISION OF THE SECRETARY.

EMBLEM OF THE WALLKILL VALLEY FARMERS' ASSOCIATION.

Announcement

1889
1899

DECADES PASS in rapid succession and the panorama of life yields little of its detail if even its outline, to the generation that follows. It is but a brief interval since the aboriginal denizens of the forests held unrestricted sway over the mountain fastnesses and intervening valleys of Southeastern New York.

It has been said that, in America, our local history has not yet received its full development. We have been careless of our traditions, monuments and relics, which, "if of a different sort from those of Europe, are no less interesting and important to preserve."

The following pages are too few to make any pretence to being a history of the Wallkill Valley. They may serve, however, to record much that might otherwise pass with the forgotten and unknown, and hence are merely offered as a contribution to the growth of local song and story "to cling like green vines about the broken fragments of the past."

The response to former publications of this character has met with such complimentary reception at home and abroad that we are encouraged to add the present volume to those of former years.

I desire to acknowledge the invaluable co-operation and assistance of the many individuals who have contributed in many ways to give this souvenir much of whatever value it may have.

W. C. Hart

SECRETARY.

THE HOMESTEAD.

"Welcome, ye pleasant dales and hills,
Where dreamlike passed my early days,
Ye cliffs and glens and laughing rills
That sing unconscious hymns of praise;
Welcome, ye woods with tranquil bowers
Embalmed in autumn's mellow sheen,
Where careless childhood gathered flowers,
And slept on mossy carpets green.

"The same bright sunlight gently plays
About the porch and orchard trees;
The garden sleeps in noontide haze,
Lulled by the murmuring of the bees;
The sloping meadows stretch away
To upland field and wooded hill;
The soft blue sky of peaceful day
Looks down upon the HOMESTEAD *still.*

"Unchanged it greets the changeful years—
Its life is one unending dream;
No record here of grief or tears;
But, like the limpid meadow stream,
It seems to sympathize with youth,
Just as the river does with age,
And ever whispers—Sweetest truth
Is written on life's title page."

Beacon Lights of the Wallkill Valley.

CORNELIA F. GILLESPIE.

OUR grand old Wallkill Valley furnishes us an almost inexhaustable supply of subject matter upon various topics, but of all topics the one most dear to our hearts is the "Beacon Lights"—the churches. These lights mean civilization and progress.

Note the rapid advancement of the people in foreign lands after the introduction of the Christian Church, then what mighty power must be ours, who are continually within its light. At almost any point along the Wallkill upon a quiet Sabbath morning one can hear some Beacon bell calling the people to the house of God. In faith our forefathers reared these blessed shrines throughout this beautiful valley to be the lights to guide our souls to the Heavenly land.

Many of those who were instrumental in rearing these houses of worship have long since passed to their final resting places. They did their work faithfully and well and are now only sleeping after a life of toil waiting for the resurrection morn, when they, with the noble ones of to-day, who would for Christ's dear sake lay down their lives, if duty demanded, will be united in that Kingdom not made with hands.

We will attempt to name and locate, as nearly as possible, the Churches in the immediate river valley. Lack of space prevents us from entering into details.

Beginning at the most northern part of the Valley near Morris Lake, Sussex Co., N. J., the source of the Wallkill, in Sparta township, in the Village of Sparta stands the First Presbyterian Church, erected in 1786. It is very prosperous, free from debt, and has a large surplus in its treasury. Present pastor is Rev. Wm. Hollinshed. The M. E. Church of Sparta was erected in 1837 and rebuilt in 1868. Present pastor is Rev. H. Bice.

About five miles northward are three churches in the Village of Ogdensburg, a Presbyterian under the pastoral care of Rev. Wm. Hollinshed of Sparta, a Baptist, and a Catholic.

Four miles to the north, on the bank of the Wallkill is the Village of Franklin Furnace. In this village a Baptist Church was built in 1832 and abandoned in 1853, but is now used by the Presbyterian congregation. Present pastor is Rev. J. K. Freed. There is also a Catholic Church here, erected in 1863, of which Father Boylan is Pastor.

Next in order is the North Church, located about two miles southwest of Hamburg, of the Presbyterian denomination, was organized from the Sparta Church (1819) and is supplied from Hamburg.

Hamburg, the next village on the Wallkill, contains four Churches—Presbyterian, organized and built in 1814, the Rev. Mr. Barnes, pastor, recently resigned; Baptist, organized in 1811, the present pastor is Rev. A.

FIRST PRESBYTERIAN CHURCH, GOSHEN, N. Y.

S. Thompson; the Church of the Good Shepherd, Rev. J. H. Smith, pastor. The first service held on June 3, 1874. It is a stone structure consisting of nave and chancel; with engaged tower, surmounted by a cross and containing a fine toned bell; and the Episcopal, completed in 1874, the Rev. J. H. Smith is present rector.

Saint Thomas' Church, Vernon, N. J., is a plain wooden building. It has a small congregation of devout people who are strongly attached to their little Church. It has a bell, pipe organ and altar hangings for the different ecclesiastical seasons. Rev. J. H. Smith, Rector.

Four miles to the north is Deckertown. This village has three churches—the First Baptist, organized in 1759, rebuilt recently, and the Rev. Bristow is its pastor; the Second Presbyterian, organized in 1834, Rev. E. A. Hamilton is present paster; and the Methodist, organized and built in 1858, the present pastor Rev. L. F. Bowman.

The Wantage M. E. Church, located three miles northeast of Deckertown and one mile west of the Wallkill is supplied from Deckertown.

PRESBYTERIAN CHURCH, RIDGEBERRY, N. Y.

Crossing the line into Orange County, eight miles northeast of Deckertown, N. J., and about two west of the Wallkill is located the pleasant village of Unionville containing three Churches — the Orange Baptist, organized in 1822, the Rev. J. King, present pastor; First Presbyterian, organized in 1803, present pastor, Rev. J. S. London; and the Methodist, organized in 1868, edifice completed in 1870, present pastor, Rev. W. S. Newsome of Westtown.

The ancient Village of Amity, a mile from Pochuck River, a tributary of the Wallkill. It rests in the center of beautiful scenery, and the Presbyterian church, which is the most conspicuous object in a wide compass, stands on an elevated site of surpassing loveliness. In the year 1797 the first church building was erected and opened for public worship, the ministerial labors of Rev. R. H. Craig, pastor since May, 1892, has grown more and more devoted as the years pass. Important improvements have been made, a pipe organ placed in the Church, and a centennial celebration was held on December 10, 1896.

Westtown, two miles west of the Wallkill in the town of Minisink, has two Churches—the Presbyterian, organized March 10, 1803, the people incorporated "The First Presbyterian Church of Westtown." Subscriptions to July, 1805, amounted to $11,733.50. September 4, 1806, the Society was taken under care of Presbytery. Rev. Thomas Grier, the first pastor, was installed February 9, 1809. One hundred and three persons were received into the communion of the church in 1815, fifty-seven in 1816, and one hundred and ninety-four in

1820, all on confession of faith. The present pastor, the Rev. R. H. Taylor, was installed May 9, 1889. The church was rebuilt near the close of the first pastorate, and remodeled under the pastorate of the Rev. D. C. Niven (1872) and again within the present pastorate (1898-9). The Methodist, organized in 1863, and the present pastor is Rev. W. S. Newsome.

The Presbyterian Church, Florida, N. Y., was organized probably in 1750. The Church has a comfortable and commodious sanctuary, beautifully situated in the center of the village. The Church is thoroughly organized. Its present membership is about 160, and its pastor the Rev. David F Bonner, D. D. The M. E. Church is supplied by Rev. F. Russell.

FIRST CONGREGATIONAL CHURCH, MIDDLETOWN.

Ridgeberry, two and one-half miles west of the Wallkill, contains two Churches—Presbyterian, organized in 1805, present pastor, Rev. T. Brittain; and a Methodist Church, pastor, Rev. R. M. Roberts.

Four miles to the north, upon the banks of the Wallkill, is the Village of Denton. This village contains a Presbyterian Church, organized in 1839.

Following the River northward from Denton, a short distance from the Wallkill, we approach the beautiful city of Middletown, which, owing to its number of Beacon Lights, ought to be very righteous. It contains fourteen Churches of which the following are the names of the organizations, each accompanied by the present pastor's name: First Presbyterian, Rev. David Winters. Second Presbyterian, Rev. Charles Beattie, D. D. The First Congregational Church, Middletown, N. Y., 1785, Rev. Charles Seeley began his pastorate. The Church had been established previous to Dec. 12, 1784. In 1786 a lot was purchased and in part is occupied by the present Church edifice; It was for forty (40) years the only Church in Middletown. 1798 Rev. W. H. Smith began efficient pastoral work; 1807 Rev. Allen Blair was chosen pastor; 1810 the ground around the Church was used for burial purposes, as it continued to be for many years. 1812 Rev. Abel Jackson was called to the pastorate, at an annual salary of $500 and 20 cords of good firewood. 1814-15 a precious revival, 125 persons uniting with the Church; 1820 Rev. Wm. Blair entered upon the pastorate of the Church; 1824 Rev. George Stebbins was called; 1825-1834 harmony did not prevail, but all disputes were finally settled; 1836 the new Church was dedicated, about the same time the first bell in Middletown was placed in the belfry of the Church. Rev. John Fishpool commenced pulpit work as a supply. 1837 Rev. M. LaCost; 1838 Rev. Chas. Machin; 1842 Rev. H. [illegible] 18[illegible] Rev. L. C. Ferritt; 1846 Rev. L. C. Lockwood. A very precious revival gave great strength to the Church; 1851 Rev. S. T. Lum, a very earnest pastor. Interior of Church greatly improved; 1854 Rev. G. T. Timlow; 1855 Rev. D. Lancaster; 1860 Rev. Jonathan Crane; 1868 pastorate of Rev. Dr. C. A. Harvey, to his indefatigable efforts was largely due the planing and erection of the present Church edifice; 1871 former house removed; 1872 corner stone of the new laid with impressive services; Oct. 22d. 1873 Church dedicated, sermon by Rev. Henry Ward Beecher, of Brooklyn Tabernacle; 1875 second pastorate of Rev. J. Crane, who died Dec. 25, 1877. A floating debt of $16,000 was cancelled; 1876 a new bell with fixtures weighing 4000 pounds, presented by Deacon W. C. McNash. An elaborate organ of great volume was purchased; 1878 Rev. F. R. Marvin, M. D. installed. 1879 entire funded and accrued debt of $21,500 paid; 1881 a large tower clock placed in the belfry of the Church; 1882 Rev. E. C. Olney called to the pastorate; 1885 Centennial of Church. $5,000 was provided to meet unpaid pledges of 1879; 1887 resignation of Rev. E. C. Olney, on account of impaired health; 1888 Rev. A. F. Pierce. Union Evangelistic services held by the Churches of the town. 106 entered into fellowship with this Church; 1889 interior of the Church was beautified and enlarged; 1892 Rev. William A. Robinson began his services as pastor. Dec. 22d. Rev. Dr. Lyman Abbott of Brooklyn, preached the sermon; 1893 resulted in placing the Church on encouraging financial basis; 1894 great spiritual results and conversions recorded; 1895 revision of Church Manual; 1896 payment of all debts resting upon the Society. During the European trip of the pastor during June and July, the pulpit was supplied by Mr. Charles P. Pierce of Yale Seminary. Grace Episcopal, Rev. David J. Evans, B. A., Rector, was incorporated Feb. 18. 1845. The present structure was begun in 1846, finished in 1847, and consecrated by Bishop Delancy, on Sept. 12, 1848. In 1866 the south transept was built by E. P. Wheeler, to whom, more than any other man, the parish is indebted for its foundation, and in the following year the north transept was added by the pious munificence of the same benefactor. The beautiful spire dates back from 1868. St. Paul's M. E., Rev. Frank L. Wilson, D. D.; First Baptist, Rev. Frank A. Heath; North St. Congregational, Rev. W. H. Morton; Prim. Old School Baptist, Elder H. C. Ker; St. Joseph's (Catholic), Rev. J. P. McClancy; Free Christian, Rev. C. M. Winchester; Christ Church (Universalist), Rev. J. Newton Emery; A. M E. Zion, Rev. J. W. McCoy; A. M. E. Bethel, Rev. T. J. Jackson; Faith Mission, Elder D. L. Conkling.

FIRST PRESBYTERIAN CHURCH, MIDDLETOWN, N. Y.

From this city we will pass on to Goshen—our own county seat, not the land of Biblical name. Herein we find five strong churches and a Presbyterian Mission (colored), of which Rev. W. C. Brown is pastor. The Presbyterian, now under the pastoral care of Rev. Robert Bruce Clark, is the oldest church in the Southern half of the valley. It was organized and had a settled pastor as early as 1721, and at present is in a very flourishing condition. The remaining four are the Methodist, Rev. W. F. Brush, pastor; Episcopal, St. James, with Rev. G. C. Betts, rector; St. John the Evangelist (Catholic), with the Rev. P. McCorry, pastor; and A. M. E. Zion, with Rev. King, pastor.

A Presbyterian Church was organized and built at Scotchtown about 1796. Rev. J. K. Mann is present pastor.

At Campbell Hall is located the First Presbyterian Church of Hampfonburg, a new edifice. This is the original [illegible]. The pastor is Rev. Alex. Gilmore.

Next in order is the Village of Montgomery, located on the east bank of the Wallkill. For the number of [illegible] is more light than her sister villages. Within the corporation are three churches. The Presbyterian, organized and built early in 1831, Rev. T. D. Elder, present pastor. The Methodist, Rev. Newton Way, pastor. The first services were held in this village about eighty years ago. Church ereected in 1829, enlarged in 1853, and thoroughly re paired and cupola built in 1860; the bell was placed in its position in 1861. The lecture room was added and colored glass windows put in in 1884. Seating capacity nearly 300. No indebtedness on the church property. And the Holy Name of Mary (Catholic), Rev. Patrick Morris, pastor.

M. E. CHURCH, GOSHEN, N. Y.

Then across the river, one mile to the West, on a high elevation, stands the historic Brick Church. Space compels the omission of details, but suffice it to say that no church can claim any nobler souls than those who have been members of this fold. The original organization (1732) was composed of German emigrants. The first structure was built of logs, the second (1760), a frame building on the present site, and the third (1803), [illegible] which was remodeled in 1834. This year (1899) the burden of debt is once more lifted from her [illegible] She is now in a prosperous condition under the pastoral care of Rev. J. F. Berg.

About two miles to the east from Montgomery village is located a Presbyterian Church, known as Goodwill. The congregation was originally comprised of emigrants from Ireland, organized about 1729. She is a prosperous Church and is now under the present care of Rev. J. H. Thompson, Montgomery, N. Y. From this Church two miles to the north-east is the Berea (Ref Dutch) Church, originally it was an off-shoot from Goodwill, organized 1819, present pastor, Rev. E. V. V. Searle, Walden, N. Y.

EPISCOPAL CHURCH, GOSHEN, N. Y.

Four miles to the north of Montgomery is the beautiful village of Walden, situated on either bank of the Wallkill. There are four Churches within the Corporation limits, viz:—The First Reformed Church, Rev. William Wyckoff Schomp, Pastor. As early as 1830 a definite effort toward establishing a Church was made, building operations began in 1835, the house was not completed till 1838. The dedication took place in August. The first pastor, Rev. John M. Scribner, was installed August 20, 1839. In 1842 Rev. Charles Whitehead became pastor, continuing till 1849. The same year Rev. Martin V. Schoonmaker became pastor, faithfully discharging his duties till 1888, almost forty years. In 1888, Rev. W. H. S. Demarest, was installed. Under his care and wise guidance, the Church was enlarged and beautified, externally and internally, as it appears to-day. During his administrations, stained glass windows were added, and electric lights and steam heat introduced. In 1897, Rev. William Wyckoff Schomp, the present incumbent, became its pastor. On account of the commanding position it occupies, it has long and favorably been known as the Hill Church. From its site the landscape, north, south, east and west is magnificent. The Highlands of the Hudson, the Shawangunk Mountains and portions of the Catskills all appear. The Wallkill River at the foot of the hill on the west flows north-ward, at times a gentle stream, and at times a raging torrent.

CATHOLIC CHURCH, GOSHEN, N. Y.

The Methodist, organized about 1820, in 1850 purchased the Covenanter Church building on Main St., present site, for their meeting house; remodeled recently, and is now a handsome edifice with a large and generous congregation, present pastor, Rev. O. Haviland. The Episcopal, (St. Andrews) organized in 1732, at St. Andrews—removed to Walden [illegible], present rector, Rev. Anketell. The Catholic edifice erected in 1894, Rev. Patrick Morris, Pastor.

[illegible] Walden three miles to the north, in the village of Wallkill, county of Ulster, near the east bank of the [illegible] the Wallkill Valley Ref. Church, edifice erected in 1869, destroyed by fire about 1889, replaced by [illegible] structure, present pastor, Rev. M. T. Conklin.

The Old Shawangunk Church, located about three miles west of Wallkill Village, was erected in 1737, and

THE HISTORIC BRICK CHURCH, MONTGOMERY, N. Y.

METHODIST EPISCOPAL CHURCH, MONTGOMERY, N. Y.

REV. M. V. SCHOONMAKER, D. D.,

Forty years pastor of the Reformed Church, Walden, N. Y.

is at present without a shepherd owing to the recent resignation of the Rev. Joseph Dixon. New Prospect Reformed Church, a daughter of the Reformed Church of Shawangunk. Feb., 1814 the Church was incorporated. The Rev. H. Polhemus was then pastor of the Church of Shawangunk, and it was the intention of both congregations that he should have the pastoral charge also of New Prospect, but before the consumation of said expectation, he was released from his earthly labors. The Rev. E. O. Moffett is the present pastor, who has received over two hundred (200) in the membership of the Church during his pastorate.

A few miles to the north from Wallkill village is the Reformed Church, New Hurley, N. Y. The first formal application for organization was Sept. 29, 1767. A second signed by fifty-two persons March 7th, 1770—formally organized Nov. 8th, 1770. During the winter of 1773-74 the first building was erected 30 x 40 ft., 1811, 20 ft. added to the rear. For forty years they were without any means of warming the building except the little foot stoves brought by these mothers of Israel. 1835 the old church was burned to the ground to give place to the present large edifice.

As a church its historical data is replete in memorable incident. Its record is of a very high order. Generations of its departed people are entombed beside the church so dear by all the hallowed associations associated with these lives. The present pastor, Rev. John A. Thurston, is deeply interested in its spiritual life, and is progressive and faithful in the development of its social and financial life.

An M. E. Church is located at [illegible] on the west side of the River nearly opposite New Hurley, the pulpit supplied having no settled pastor.

Guilford Church, a short distance west of Gardiner was erected in [illegible], the present pastor is Rev. [illegible] Fisher, [illegible], Ulster Co., N. Y.

A R. C. Church of recent construction [illegible] Gardiner village, Rev. [illegible] is its pastor [illegible] the St. Charles Catholic [illegible] Rev. John B. McGrath is present pastor.

WALLKILL VALLEY REFORMED CHURCH.

PRESBYTERIAN CHURCH, CAMPBELL HALL, N. Y.

PRESBYTERIAN CHURCH, GOODWILL, N. Y.

REFORMED CHURCH, NEW HURLEY, N. Y.

In the village of New Paltz are three churches, viz.: Methodist, with Rev. R. L. Ross, pastor, and the Reformed. The latter originally French Ref., was organized 1683; the French language was used until 1733; then the Dutch until 1800. The audience room of the present edifice is very spacious. The church numbers 272 families and has 576 communicants, and is the largest church in the Classis of Kingston. The Rev. E. C. Oggel, D. D., is the pastor.

African M. E. Zion, Rev. C. H. Williams, pastor, organized Oct. 1858, at Clintondale; 1860 removed to New Paltz; rebuilt 1875. Membership 150; 40th anniversary, Oct. 16 and 17, 1898.

At Rosendale are three churches: the Reformed, organized and erected in 1843, with Rev. Wm. Coombs as present pastor; an Episcopal, with Rev. Henry Barker, rector, and the St. Peters' (Catholic) with Rev. P. F. Woodham, pastor.

Rosendale Plains Reformed Church is under the pastoral care of Rev. Wm. Coombs.

Bloomingdale Ref., organized in 1796, erected 1797, and St. Remy, erected in 1864, are both under the pastoral care of Rev. J. Millet, Whiteport, N. Y.

The St. Patrick's Church (Catholic) of Whiteport, has Rev. F. M. Fagan for pastor.

M. E. CHURCH, WALDEN, N. Y.

Dashville Falls or Rifton Glen Ref. Church, was erected in 1831, and is at present without a pastor.

We now arrive at the north end of our Valley, with Kingston as the terminating point. This beautiful city contains twenty-eight organized churches, of which the following are the names, each accompanied by the name of the pastor, viz: First Baptist, Rev. Philip B. Strong; First Baptist (Rondout), Rev. H. W. Sherwood; Bethany Chapel, Rev. ——; Jewish Congregation, Rev. Benuet Grad, Rabbi; Jewish Congregation, Rev. David Goldberg, Rabbi; English Lutheran Church of Redeemer, Kingston, N. Y., organized January 24th, 1897, with 184 charter members; present membership, 298; Sunday School organized June, 1897, enrollment, 232; Luther League (Young People's Society), membership 46; Ladies' Aid Society, membership 103. Wm. F. [illegible], pastor. Value of property, $8,000. German Lutheran, Rev. A. Schinidtkonz; German Lutheran, Rev. G. A. Henkee; Methodist Episcopal, Rev. E. L. Hoffecker; Methodist Episcopal (St. James), Rev. B. C. Warren; Methodist Episcopal, Rev. Arthur Thompson; Methodist Episcopal (African) Rev. C. C. Ringgold; Methodist Episcopal (Colored), Rev. Edw. Scarboro; Presbyterian, Rev. C. S. Stowitts; Presbyterian, Rev. J. F. Williamson; Protestant Episcopal, Rev. Thos. Burrows; Protestant Episcopal (Supply), Rev. Alden Bennett; Church of the Holy Cross, Rev. C. M. Hall; First Church of Christ (Scientist), Rev. —— 22 Franklin St; First Reformed (Dutch), (1661), Rev. J. G. Van Slyke; Second Reformed (Dutch), (1848), Rev. T. B. Seeley; Reformed Church of the Comforter (1770), Rev. S. E. Winnie; Roman Catholic, Rev. Francis Fabian; Roman Catholic, Rev. D. P. Ward; Roman Catholic, Rev. R. L. Burtsell; Roman Catholic, Rev. E. M. Sweeney; Roman Catholid, Rev. M. Kueken; Union Children's Church, Rev. ——.

REV. JOHN A. THURSTON, NEW HURLEY, N. Y.

The First Reformed Church of Kingston is undoubtedly the oldest organization in the Valley, around which cluster many historic memories. The early settlers with the dauntless spirit and Holland courage, settling as early as 1665, near Kingston, at the mouth of the Wallkill, were earnest and devoted in their religion. Their names have become a synonym for stern morality on ardent church lines. The ruling passion seemed the love of Church and God. Faith to them was more than the homeland, and their sturdy religion became rich heritage of their new country. These factors, touched and entwined together making and transmitting still each its element of [illegible] that close together in this very valley of the Wallkill, to this day betray their lineage. The first church was erected in 1661, at the corner of what is now known as Main and Wall Sts. It was built of logs and [illegible] in 1679 a stone building was erected, and the church was incorporated in 1719. The interior of this building was consumed by fire, when Kingston was burned in 1777; the building remained standing [illegible]. A stone building was again erected; this has been supplanted by the present modern structure erected [illegible].

Note.—We are indebted to Mr. Charles E. Stickney of Deckertown, N. J., for data and information relating to [illegible] south of Goshen.

Our Valley contains many religious denominations, but only those who accept Christ as their chief corner stone, may expect a Union of Creeds in Heaven as there are no Sects in that Holy place. What a grand life it would be if we could all

THE OLD KINGSTON DUTCH REFORMED CHURCH.

"So live, that when our summons comes to join
The innumerable caravan which moves
To that mysterious realm where each shall take
His chamber in the silent halls of death,
Go not like the quarry slave at night,
Scourged to his dungeon; but, sustained and soothed
By an unfaltering trust, approach the grave
Like one who wraps the drapery of his couch
About him, and lies down to pleasant dreams."

The Huguenot Memorial House, New Paltz, N. Y.

ALFRED HARCOURT.

THE old colonial building, widely known as the Hasbrouck house, has recently been purchased by the Huguenot Patriotic, Historical, Monumental Society of New Paltz, for the purpose of preserving it, both on account of its historic interest, and because of its suitability as a place for the storing of historic documents and ancestral relics.

The old, steep-roofed homestead, which is full of interest to any one who takes pride in a Huguenot ancestry, was erected in 1712, and with the exception of the DuBois house, which has lost much of its historic interest through being remodeled, it was and is the finest of the seven homesteads erected by the patentees and their children.

The first point of interest about the Hasbrouck house is that it is entirely hand made. The nails were hammered out by the village blacksmith, and the boards were planed by the home carpenter. The wide chimneys, made to receive the large sticks of firewood without splitting, were built of bricks brought from Holland to Kingston, and drawn from there to New Paltz over the primitive roads of two centuries ago.

THE HUGUENOT MEMORIAL HOUSE NEW PALTZ, N. Y.

The rooms of the lower floor on the north side were originally used as a store. Here were kept the few necessities of the early settlers, and here also from time to time liquor was sold. The bar, a large slab of wood, was placed across one corner of the room from the chimney to the window sills. On it is s till "chalked up" a genuine account of a [illegible] rum. Near the chimney is a closet which might easily escape notice and which, itis said, was used as a money drawer. There are two other rooms on the lower floor which were used as living rooms by the family and which were large and commodious for a house of that time. The family rooms on the second floor are of good size, and the heavy beams and slanting ceilings give them a truly colonial appearance.

The [illegible] of the movement which resulted in the purchase of the house this winter, was made in April, [illegible]. Until his recent death, the late Edmund Elting was an earnest and prominent worker in the matter, [illegible] in the capacity of secretary.

The present officers of the society are: President, Ralph LeFevre; First Vice-President, Jesse Elting; [illegible] W. Elting; Treasurer, Jacob M. Hasbrouck. The trustees of the society are Louis Bevier, A. [illegible] M. Sharpe, Irving Elting, Frank Hasbrouck, Joseph E. Hasbrouck, Jesse Elting, Jacob LeFevre, [illegible] DuBois, Abram D. Brodhead and Jacob M. Hasbrouck.

Joseph Brant, the Chief of the Mohawks, who commanded at the Battle of Minisink.

BY HARRISON W. NANNY.

JOSEPH BRANT—TAYENDANEGEA is a household name in Orange county, and he who bore it looms a dark lurid figure against the background of our Revolutionary history. A pure blooded Mohawk, his education and training was had in the schools of the white man. In the fierce warfare which England waged to coerce her rebellious colonies into obedience, his part has been much misunderstood. He was never, in any sense of the word, a border ruffian, nor is he to be reckoned of the ilk of those who, within the memory of men hardly beyond middle age, made the term a reproach in the Kansas-Missouri trouble, just prior to the Civil War.

On the contrary Brant was a Christian and a member of the Episcopal Church and aided in the translation of the Prayer Book, the Acts of the Apostles and Catechism into the Mohawk tongue. One of the earliest recorded incidents concerning him is by Rev. Dr. Wheelock, a clergyman in the Mohawk valley, in which he says "that in the French War Brant went out with a company against the Indians, (these were allies of the French) in which he behaved so much like the christian and the soldier, that he gained great esteem."

He was presented at the court of the king in London, and was the friend of Boswell. His portrait, painted in 1776, has been preserved at Warwick, and a copy of same accompanies this sketch.

When the trouble between England and the Colonies began, he was urged to remain neutral, but refused. He asserted that his race was bound by the faith pledged in ancient treaties to their great father, the king, who had defended them against the French, in the struggle for the dominion over this continent, to aid him against his enemies, and he loyally kept that pledge. But the hand on the dial was not to be turned backward. In the providence of God a new nation was to have birth, in which crowns, scepters and royalty were to have no place, and Joseph Brant was to be put down on the record by the troubled colonists as the most blood-thirsty and cruel of those who sought to compel their obedience to law and an established government. To this belief the disaster at Minisink, which brought death to many a Goshen family, in a no small degree contributed. But it is not so. War is not humane, "war is hell," and the part acted by Joseph Brant as a commander of men in armed hostility to other men acting from a different point of view, can in no wise be considered as more culpable than that of Grant or Sherman. To him, as well as to them, is laid no charge of personal cruelty or rapine. Some of the followers of each, we know, left behind them a trail dishonorable to human instincts, and to whom either of the three commanders would have meted death as the penalty, if the offender were known.

The massacre at Wyoming was mainly at the hands of white men, yet the same has been laid at the door of Brant, and Campbell, in his "Gertrude of Wyoming," sings:

"The Mammoth comes—the foe—the Monster Brant—
With all his howling desolating band."

A cherished tradition of one of the oldest families in Orange county—the Fullerton—relates of an ancestress, Mary Whittaker, who at the age of twelve years escaped the slaughter at Wyoming, thus: (Eager is quoted page 414) "Brant took her by the hair of the head and held her up by one hand and painted her face with red paint with the other and then let her go, telling her that was the mark of safety." On the same occasion, (Eager is again quoted, page 415) "A little boy, John Finch, also an Orange county ancestor, was saved without being painted. This little boy laughed at the odd and grotesque appearance of the Indians, and one raised his tomahawk to strike him down. Brant saw the motion of the Indian, seized and ordered him not to in-

pare the boy." While in both these incidents is found the kernel of that which the after-time has conceded [to Brant, his gentleness and humane disposition, it is necessary to dispel this romance of these two old families. If any one fact has been established in history, it is that Brant was not at Wyoming, and the poet Campbell, in the notes to the second edition of "Gertrude of Wyoming," remarks that "since writing the poem I have had access to documents which completely satisfy me that Brant was not at that scene of desolation." And adds, "I also ascertained that Brant strove to mitigate the cruelty of Indian warfare, and his name remains in the poem a pure and declared character of fiction."

JOSEPH BRANT—TAYENDANEGEA.
[illegible] Six Nations, from the original painting in [illegible] the Earl of Warwick, Eng.

An incident, not unlike those above noted, is preserved in the tradition of the Van Auken school-house. During the raid of 1779, at Minisink, the girls stood lamenting around the dead body of their teacher, and bemoaning their own coming doom, when a strong muscular Indian suddenly came along and with a brush dashed some black paint across their aprons, as the symbol of safety. "This (Eager is being quoted, page 389) was Brant, and the little daughters of the settlers were saved." These girls impressed the paint upon the boys and they too were passed unharmed.

In the official report made of the battle of Minisink, among other absurdities, it is gravely asserted that Brant carried off a number of children as prisoners. Happily, for the truth of history as well as humanity's sake, a prisoner, the only one captured, Capt. John Wood, of the Goshen company of Col. Tusten's regiment, left behind him a journal of the events following the battle, and his journey while a captive with Capt. Brant, as he terms him, and those under him, to the Indian country, which disposes of the question to the contrary. And this journal well sustains Brant's official report of the Minisink raid and battle, in which he says, "we in no wise injured women or children."

It is the desire of the author of this monograph to refrain from any discussion of the Minisink battle, as that properly belongs to a work now in course of preparation for the publisher.

Yet it may be remarked that, since Goshen's first commemoration of that event, which was the subject of an article in the Souvenir of 1898, much has been brought out which reveals a tale of the cowardice and flight of a portion of the forces which marched to oppose Brant, and which in numbers exceeded those of the latter, and thus left the Goshen regiment to annihilation.

Another incident, and as characteristic of Brant, is preserved in a letter written by him to Gen. Van Rensselaer, which accompanied a returned captive girl, in which he says: "I send you by one of my runners, the

VALLEY AND STREAM, ESSEX COUNTY, N. J.

child, which he will deliver that you may know that whatever others may do, I do not make war on women and children. I am sorry to say that I have those engaged with me in the service who are more savage than the savages themselves." A sad commentary of the red man upon the Tory.

"Historical accuracy is a plant of slow growth," says a historical writer. The same might be observed concerning biography. Washington is asserted to have been a Christian, a man of prayer. That Howe, Clinton, Burgoyne and Cornwallis were followers of the Divine Master, no American historian has yet put upon the record. Praying Generals always belong to the same side as their biographers. Brant has had no biographer of his race or blood, yet a white historian has written that Brant, prominent among those of his day, was devoted to christianizing, civilizing and uplifting his race, and declared himself as having always striven to avoid the unnecessary shedding of blood, and to avert the cruelties incident to war.

Three generations have been upon the stage since Joseph Brant ceased to be a factor among the affairs of the living. The fury of political passion which marked his era is dead: the bitterness engendered by the loss through war, of the results of years of labor to the border settlers, has been obliterated by the county which years of peace has brought to their descendants, and to these there lingers only the tradition

"Of far off unhappy things,
And battles long ago."

Prejudice has been yielding to the results of calm and cold historical research and investigation, and an impartial judgment can now be rendered by the tribunal sitting at the dawn of the twentieth century, a decision which for fairness, was impossible to be accorded during the years so closely allied with the events, of which the bitter memories had not passed away.

St. Andrews.

MISS MAY HUNT.

THIS quiet peaceful hamlet is located in the northwest corner of the Town of Montgomery on a patent of 3,000 acres, granted to Henry Wileman in the year 1709, within the then County of Ulster. The hamlet is rich in tradition and interest, being one of the oldest within the present borders of Orange.

Mr. Wileman was the first settler and divided the patent into lots in 1712. The settlement adopted his name and was known as Wilemantown. His nationality was Irish. He was a Free Mason and a lawyer, the first admitted to practice (1727) in Orange Co. It was upon his land in 1774 that Log Church was erected and a plot of land adjoining set aside as a burial place. The property is now owned by Mr. George Dunn, and the location was in the corner of the field on the fork of the roads leading from St. Andrews to Walden and Wallkill. He was a benefactor of the church, and it is here in the old yard that his dust reposes with that of many other early settlers.

It is a much to be lamented fact that all vestige of this ancient, burial place should have been destroyed over half a century ago.

Under the pastoral care of the Rev. John Sayre in the year 1770, Log Church became incorporated under the name of St. Andrews, and a new edifice erected in the southeast of St. Andrews Cemetery. The hamlet then assumed the church name, and it was here that the family of Lieutenant Governor Colden attended worship. A visit to the cemetery which adjoined the church reveals the fact that it has served as a burial place for over a century and a quarter.

Here rest the remains of the Dorcases', Galation's, Banks', Gee's and Graham's. Capt. George Graham being interred 1774 families all connected with the early history of the church. Here also we find the graves of heroes of the Revolutionary and the Civil War. Peace to their ashes, and let us hope that this (God's Acre) may never share the fate of the old Episcopal yard.

Previous to the location of the new church, a number of buildings had been erected. The principal ones being a school house built of mud and logs, located on the old road leading to King's Hill, opposite the present residence of Mr. Chauncey Radiker, a tavern on the brink of the brook and a store. Here also was established one of the first Post Offices of the county.

St. Andrews is not lacking in bloody historical events. It was here that an Indian massacre took place at the beginning of the French and Indian war. Gen. Clinton as Captain was engaged in the attack, and seventeen Indians were killed. Again at the beginning of the Revolution, Lieutenant Governor Colden came very near being shot by the indignant Whigs as he attempted to read the King's decree. South of the hamlet in front of the residence of Mr. Corsey, is the site of an Indian fort, and to the west of the village during the winter of 1782, a company of Revolutionary soldiers laid encamped. It was while acting as a special messenger from this encampment to the Commander-in-chief at Newburgh, that John McLean afterward Commissary General of this State, was attacked, taken from his horse, gagged, tied to a tree and the papers referring to his errand taken. He was rescued the following morning.

We still find many of the descendants of the old colonial families here. Arthur McKinney located here in 1745, and a portion of his original tract is still owned and occupied by his great-great-grand-son. Soon after came the Beattie's, Snyder's, Kidd's, McKissock's, Coe's and Crowell's—descendants of which are still numerous about the village. Robert Crowell purchased the King's Hill farm, then a wilderness, about 1771, from the St. Andrews Church.

Approximate to the village is the old stone house built previous to the Revolution, occupied by Mr. Charles Thorne. Four generations of the Thorne family family have been born in this house.

Hence many other points of interest to be gleaned by the local historian, of which space here is to limited to mention.

"THE SUNSHINE OF THE VALLEY."

RESIDENCE OF REV. ROBERT H. McCREADY, CHESTER, N. Y., A FORMER PASTOR OF THE HISTORIC BRICK CHURCH, MONTGOMERY, N. Y.

Rev. Robert Houston McCready, Ph. D.

REV. ROBERT HOUSTON MCCREADY, PH. D., was born at Pittsburgh, Pa., July 12, 1853. At the age of fourteen his father died, and in that same year he began life for himself as a store boy. At sixteen he made a public confession of faith, and became a member of the church. He received the average English education at the public schools, later he studied under Prof. Love. He graduated from the Western University of Pennsylvania, June, 1870. One preparatory and three college years were spent in West Geneva College, Ohio. Previous to his University course, he spent the required four years in the Alleghany Seminary, and graduated in the summer of 1883. He received calls from New Castle, Pa., New Concord, O., Oil City, Pa., Barnesville, N. B., and Coldenham, N. Y., accepting the latter, March 6, 1884. Later he filled pastorates at Prospect Hill, Eighty Second St. near Park Ave., N. Y. In 1890 he accepted the pastorate of the Old Brick Church at Montgomery.

He was married to Miss Bell H. Beattie, daughter of Rev. David Beattie of Scotchtown, N. Y., June 21, 1888.

The writer of this sketch is fully acquainted with his earnest zeal in his ministry at Coldenham and Montgomery—of the good fellowship existing between pastor and people, and his watchful care over the interests of the community at large. His name is honored and revered among the citizens of the Valley of the Wallkill. Mr. McCready is the pastor of the First Presbyterian Church, at Chester, N. Y.

Rev. Robert Bruce Clark.

THE REV. ROBERT BRUCE CLARK has been pastor of the historic Goshen Church since January 1st, 1886, and is the successor of the Rev. Dr. Snodgrass, who in his day was amongst the famous Presbyterian divines, and was settled at Goshen during the last thirty-six years of his venerable life. Mr. Clark is a graduate of Amherst College, Union Seminary, and is identified with various interests of the beautiful village in which he lives. The Presbyterian Church of Goshen was organized in the year 1720. Three edifices have been used by the congregation since that time. The first was built sometime between 1720 and 1730; the second was built in 1812; and the present commanding structure was dedicated 1871. It is massive, commodious, beautiful for situation, of solid, rough stone to the top of its spire of 186 feet, comfortably seating 1,200 people, and in the midst of a large and beautiful park in the centre of the village. The 175th anniversary of the church was celebrated in the Spring of 1895.

Charles Edward Millspaugh.

CHARLES EDWARD MILLSPAUGH was born on the homestead, in the town of Goshen. Educated at the Farmers' Hall Academy, Goshen, graduating from that institution. Six years were spent in the employ of W. L. Vail, a merchant of Florida, N. Y. A partnership was formed under the firm name of Merriam & Millspaugh, in the village of Goshen, in 1860, engaging in the general dry goods business, which continued until 1872, being then dissolved by mutual consent. Mr. Millspaugh immediately entered into partnership with D. Redfield, under the firm name of Redfield & Millspaugh, continuing until the death of Mr. Redfield, since which time the business has been conducted by Mr. Millspaugh.

Few men are more useful or prominent in church work. For many years he has filled the position of trustee of the Goshen Presbyterian Church, with the office of Clerk and Treasurer, and Chairman of several important committees of the Church. For more than twenty years he has been the honored Superintendent of the Sunday School, and is the best known and most prominent Sunday School worker in the county, frequently serving as President of the Orange County Sunday School Association, organized May 22, 1861.

The writer of this sketch was intimately associated with Mr. Millspaugh in this work for a period of ten years, and can attest to the great services rendered, which resulted in the general revival of Sunday School interest throughout the county.

When the limitations of this life is reached, when the tabernacle of the body is broken, like the jar that holds the roses, though broken in fragments, the perfume of the roses lingers, so the memory of a good and useful life will cling like green vines about the broken fragments of the past.

Rev. J. H. Thompson.

REV. J. H. THOMPSON was born at Bemis Heights, New York, April 28, 1862. He prepared for college at The Hudson River Institute, at Claverack, New York, from which he graduated in 1883. In the fall of the same year he entered Hamilton College, at Clinton, New York, and graduated in the class of '87. He entered Princeton Theological Seminary in the fall of 1887, and graduated in 1890. He was ordained to the Gospel Ministry by the Presbytery of Troy, New York, in May 1890; and entered temporarily in home mission work in Northern Idaho. On September 1, 1890, he was married to Miss S. Cornelia Lansing, daughter of the Rev. A. G. Lansing of the Reformed Church. In the spring of 1891, he was called to the pastorate of the Goodwill Presbyterian Church of Montgomery, New York, where he still remains.

John G. Howell.

THE father of the subject this sketch was a native of the old town of Goshen, where he was born in1797. His father, Silas Howell, was one of the many early emigrants from Long Island, who, in themselves and their descendants, have so largely contributed to the substantial elements of our country's population and worth. He removed from Goshen to Newburgh with his father, and located on the Newburgh and Cochecton Turnpike, and in that vicinity he spent nearly the whole of his long and worthy life of 85 years among the notable sons of Orange County, which to enumerate them would be legion. The subject of our sketch is the younger son of R. and O. Belknap Howell, born July 23d, 1829, on the farm where he now resides, being a man of sterling character, keeping abreast of the times by strictly attending to the business of agriculture, with a desire to make two blades of grass grow where one grew before. He is eminently successful in his business, and is one of the well-to-do men of the town. He has been a member of the Goodwill Church for 30 years, and trustee for about 15 years. His family consist of two children, David B. Howell and Sarah Francis Howell. Both are married and have homes of their own.

Rev. William Wyckoff Schomp.

REV. WILLIAM WYCKOFF SCHOMP, the youngest son of David G. and Phebe A. (Todd) Schomp, was born on his father's farm, near Bedminster, Somerset County, N. J. He is of Holland descent—the first of his name coming to this country in 1672 and settling in Bushwick, Long Island; he is thus entitled to be and is a member of the Holland Society of New York.

He prepared for college at Rev. William Cornell's Classical Institute, Somerville, N. J. After passing the June examinations, he entered Rutger's College at New Brunswick, N. J., in the fall of 1872, graduating in June, 1876. Having had the ministry in view before entering college, he became a student in the Theological Seminary and graduated from that institution in May, 1879. After a summer's rest, he accepted a call to become the pastor of the Reformed Church of Glenham, Dutchess County, N. Y., and began his work there November 16, 1879. His pastorate at Glenham was noted, like each succeeding one, for harmonious, quiet work, and the forming of most delightful friendships. The first pastorate closed November 8, 1885, under conditions similar to those with which each succeeding pastorate has ended, viz., with an urgent call to another field and earnest solicitations to remain in his present charge. Having received and accepted a call to become the pastor of the Reformed Churches of Marbletown (Stone Ridge, N. Y.), and North Marbletown, Ulster Co., N. Y., he began his labors in his new charge November 15, 1885. After a successful and laborious term of seven years' service with those churches, he resigned to accept a call to the First Reformed Church of Athens, Greene Co., N. Y., and commenced his service with that church January 8, 1893. He was installed as pastor of the Reformed Church at Walden September 1, 1897, preaching his first sermon on the following Sunday (5th).

Henry Suydam.

HENRY SUYDAM was born on Long Island in 1826, son of Moses and Mary Schoonmaker Suydam, whose early ancestors all came from Holland. He was educated in Brooklyn, graduated under Doctor Campbell, who later, became Professor of the Theological Seminary of New Brunswick, N. J. The occupation of his early life, was raising produce for New York markets. In 1852 he married Lemma Anna, daughter of Henry Bergen of Long Island, later, of Orange County. In 1854, while visiting with his uncle, the late Rev. M. V. Schoonmaker of Walden, he decided to locate in the Wallkill Valley, and bought the farm of the late Joseph Hasbrouck Decker, two miles south of Walden, where he continued farming for thirty-five years, bringing his farm to a high state of cultivation—after which time, his four children being married, he retired from farming, coming to the village of Walden where he and his wife reside with their youngest daughter, Mary Ella, wife of T. D. Barker. After coming to Orange County he became an active member of the Reformed Church at Walden, serving for many successive years as an Elder. In 1860, the Wallkill Valley Cemetery Association was formed, he being one of the trustees, and continued a trustee until 1888, when he was elected its President, and has since then devoted much of his time personally, overseeing and helping to beautify the city of the dead. In 1888, about twenty-five additional acres were bought, and have since been paid for by the Cemetery Association, and at the present time, are undergoing extensive improvements, it being the aim of the Association to make it one of the finest cemeteries in Orange County.

James T. Irwin.

JAMES T. IRWIN was born in the town of Montgomery, January 14th, 1830, the youngest son of the late Edward Irwin and Rachael Traphagen, and grandson of John Irwin of Revolutionary fame, his father being a farmer. He acquired some knowledge of farm life until 1845, when he removed to Newburgh, and learned the trade of a carriage trimmer, in which business he is engaged at No. 7 South Water Street, Newburgh, N. Y. In June, 1852, Mr. Irwin married Miss Catharine La Tour of Newburgh. Mrs. irwin died April 3, 1863. He was again married to Miss Prudence McMunn, of Newburgh, October 19, 1865. Mr. Irwin has been a member of Trinity M. E. Church for the past fifty years, and for many years a member of the official board of the church. He is a member of Highland Lodge of Odd Fellows, and is a past Noble Grand, and past District Deputy Grand Master of Orange District, No. 1. Mr. Irwin is an active and earnest worker in the Order, in which he takes much pride. He is frequently called upon to deliver addresses at public meetings of the order in Newburgh, as well as in other places, and is well and favorably known to the past and present Grand Officers of the State.

James W. Barnes. 1417553

JAMES W. BARNES was born at Middle Hope, Orange Co., N. Y., April 15th, 1859, and passed his boyhood days on the farm of his parents, Nathaniel and Martha Waring Barnes. He obtained his early education at the district school at that place, afterward attending the Newburgh Academy, finishing with a special course at W. L. Chapman's private school. He began his business life by accepting the employment of Gillies & Needam, afterwards Gillies, Needam & Sands, February 1st, 1876, continuing with them until September 1st, 1880, when the firm was dissolved. Mr. Sands withdrew to form a partnership with Mr. Barnes, under the firm name of Sands & Barnes, which started in the general dry goods business at the present location No. 99 Water Street, and continued five years. Mr. Barnes succeeding to the business, formed a partnership with his brother-in-law, Mr. W. N. Owen, which continued for one year, since which time he has conducted the business alone. He married Miss Sarah F. Owen, March 29th, 1882. They have one son, N. Waring Barnes, who has just taken his examinations for admission to Columbia University, New York City. Mr. Barnes has been prominently identified with Trinity M. E. Church for a long time. He has been assistant superintendent of the Sunday School, Steward, and for the last eight years a member of the Board of Trustees. Mr. Barnes is a man of uncommon common sense, of dignified and polite demeanor. He is kindly in spirit, is true as steel to his friends. He is tireless in his integrity—he is incompatible in his integrity. He has business ability, has good business habits, commanding the esteem of his fellows, and deserves the success with which he has been favored.

George B. Harris.

GEORGE B. HARRIS, the youngest son of George F. Harris and Eveline Youngblood, was born near Pine Bush, N. Y. After graduating at the public school, he attended the Albany Business College, and entered his brother's store at Ballville, N. Y., and conducted the same for several years. April, 1898, he succeeded James S. Eaton in an old established business at Walden, N. Y., where Mr. Harris now conducts an extensive grocery store. September, 189[illegible], at Circleville, N. Y., he married Miss Minnie W. Shaw, daughter of Robert W. Shaw. Mr. Harris is a member of the Reformed Church at Bloomingburgh, N. Y., and of the Masonic Lodge of Walden.

Alex. Goldberg.

ALEX. GOLDBERG, of whom the above is a strikingly good likeness, was born in Kingston, N. Y., in 1861, and at the age of four years removed with his parents to Poughkeepsie. He was educated in the public schools at the latter place, and entered the clothing business at the age of 15 years, and removed to Newburgh in 1882, where he was engaged in the same line as partner, and finally sole owner of the recognized leading establishment of the city. In the winter of 1897-'98, he removed his business to the store No. 83-85 Water Street—a much larger and more modern building, where he now conducts an establishment without a peer between New York and Albany, and prides himself as an Outfitter for man or boy, and greatly enlarged the scope of his business. The mammoth show windows of Mr. Goldberg's store are one of the attractions of the city. He has always been accredited as one of the city's most substantial and enterprising business men, with the interests of his adopted city uppermost in all his efforts. He is prominently identified with social and fraternal interests in the city, and his intelligence and good fellowship make him a popular citizen with many warm, personal friends.

John Schwartz.

AMONG the prominent citizens of German birth in the city of Poughkeepsie, N. Y., none holds a higher place in the estimation of the community than the gentleman whose name introduces this sketch. He is extensively engaged in the tobacco business, and has an enviable reputation for integrity and fair dealing as well as for thrift and enterprise.

Mr. Schwartz was born in Bavaria, Germany, September 9th, 1839. His father, John Schwartz, died when our subject was a child; when ten years of age he came with his mother to New York City. In January, 1850, they came to Poughkeepsie, and after attending school for a short time, he entered the cigar business, which he has made his life work.

On May 6th, 1860, Mr. Schwartz married Miss Bayer, a native of Troy, N. Y. They have four children, all sons. On May 1st, 1861, he succeeded Mr. Joseph Bayer, his father-in-law, in the business of manufacturing cigars and tobaccos. This business is now carried on, in greatly enlarged proportions by Mr. Schwartz and three sons, constituting the firm of John Schwartz & Sons, they having become partners February 1st, 1889.

Adam Wiley.

THE subject of this sketch, Mr. Adam Wiley, was born at Croton Falls, Westchester County, New York, on the 9th day of May, 1849, his father being James Wiley and his mother Rebecca Ritchie.

Several years of Mr. Wiley's early life were spent at school at Croton Falls, N. Y., and Mill Plains, Ct., but, his father dying when he was fourteen years of age, without leaving any means of support for a large family, young Adam found it necessary to discontinue his school career and seek remunerative employment.

The first few years of his new venture were spent at farming, but learning of a position open in one of the livery stables in Brewster, and as his mind possessed a natural bent for horses, he made application and procured the situation. His employment here lasted five years, and during that time he had an opportunity to study veterinary under Dr. Amos Smith, a then well known veterinarian. The instruction thus received has proved of such value to Mr. Wiley, that he has won a meritorious record as a highly competent doctor of horses and cattle, and for which proficiency he was recently awarded a Diploma by the N. Y. State Board of Regents.

For the past twenty-two years Mr. Wiley has worked for the Borden interests, and for the last fourteen years he has been employed directly by the Borden family, the latter five years of which, as superintendent at "Home Farm."

On November 8th, 1873, he was joined in marriage with Rebecca Sweetman, of Brewster, Putnam County, New York, and as a result of such union, there were four sons and two daughters, three sons and one daughter still living.

James L. Crawford.

JAMES L. CRAWFORD, the subject of this sketch, was born at Searsville, Orange County, N. Y. He developed much mechanical skill early in life, and when his school days were passed, naturally chose the carpenter's trade, at which he made very rapid progress, and soon had the reputation of being a very skillful and proficient workman, which naturally led to his rapid advancement in his chosen work, now extending over four decades. In 1870 Mr. Crawford became a resident of Walden, since which date he has been largely identified with its building interests. He built the Episcopal Church at Walden, constructed the tall spire on the Brick Church at Montgomery, and at different periods made many extensive repairs and additions to the New York and Walden Knife Works. He has erected a great many of the residences of Walden and its environs. Mr. Crawford has always been a loyal Republican and an earnest and effective worker in behalf of his party. He served as town Assessor for a term of years, and filled the position in a fair and impartial manner. For about thirty years he has been a member of the Odd Fellows, and has passed the chairs, is prominent in the order of the K. of P., and a representative citizen of the Valley of the Wallkill.

James R. McCullough.

JAMES R. MCCULLOUGH, whose portrait is given above, is a native of the Wallkill Valley, being born near Walden, April 25th, 1839, and contiuued to live there (with brief intervals) until September, 1887, when he removed with his family to Newburgh where he still resides. Mr. McCullough spent many years of his life in the grocery business in or near Walden. In 1870 he was appointed U. S. Census Enumerator for the towns of Montgomery and Crawford, and for the five years following was employed by J. S. Taylor & Co., lumber and coal dealers. He is and always has been an ardent Republican, was twice elected Collector of the Town of Montgomery, and for many years was elected Clerk of the Board of Trustees of the village, also Inspector of Election for the town. He was active in the Fire Department, being a member since 1860; he was a charter member of Enterprise Steamer Co., when it was organized in 1872, and his name still appears on their roll of honorary members. He joined Freeman's Lodge, No. 170, I. O. O. F. in 1863, filled all the different chairs in the Lodge, and was chosen in 1876, D. D. G. M. for the District then comprising the counties of Orange and Sullivan, containing seventeen Lodges. He was a charter member of Orange Lodge, No. 2470, Knights of Honor, and the first Dictator of the Lodge, and being a veteran of the Civil War, was a charter member of Fairchild Post, No. 564, G. A. R., and is at present a member of Newburgh Lodge, No. 309, F. & A. M. Mr. McCullough is now, and has been for some years employed by the Board of Public Works of the City of Newburgh, as Assistant Superintendent of Streets. In his leisure moments he still takes great interest in the fraternal, religious and political organizations of his adopted home.

Philip Ayers.

Wesley Wait, D. D. S.

WESLEY WAIT, D. D. S., was born near Montgomery, N. Y., May 15th, 1861, son of Thomas and Mary Mould Wait. He received his education at the district school and Montgomery Academy. In 1881 he entered New York College of Denistry, and eight months after was appointed first assistant to Professor J. B. Littig. In 1883 he graduated one year ahead of his class, his degree not being conferred until 1884, and began the practice of his profession at Newburgh in 1885. He is the proprietor of the Consumers Ice Company, now leased to the Muchattoes Lake Ice Company, also of the Newburgh Floral Company, having store on Second Street and greenhouses at West Newburgh, which contain thirty thousand feet of glass. He still practices the profession of denistry. From 1890 to 1893 he represented New York State in the American Association of Inventors and Manufacturers, and in 1891 represented this Congressional District at the Patent Centennial at Washington, D. C., being the inventor and owner of several valuable inventions. In 1885 Mr. Wait was married to Emily S. Rawlins, youngest daughter of General John H. Rawlins, chief of staff to General U. S. Grant, and ex-Secretary of War. Mrs. Wait died March 25, 1897, leaving one child, a daughter, Lucille R. His residence is on Grand Avenue, Balmville, N. Y.

Harrison Wheeler Nanny.

HARRISON WHEELER NANNY, whose monograph of Brant appears in this annual of the Souvenir, is a well-known Goshen lawyer. Beside his reputation as such, he is reckoned by the "canny kin" as their congener in classical and literary scholarship, also being conceded a foremost place among the younger historians of Orange county. His many addresses before historical and literary societies and on occasions of public ceremonies, have won high encomiums from critical scholars and historians. Mr. Nanny was born in the town of Warwick where his family settled long prior to the Revolution. He received the baccalaureate degree at Union College where he graduated in the class of 1868, and immediately began the study of the law. He is of direct Welsh descent and of family devoted for generations to the profession of arms. His ancestor Capt. John Nanny raised a company, in the year 1645, for service against King Charles I, which was captured at Dolgelly, North Wales, and had presented to him the alternative of a political trial or an embarkation to America. Each succeeding generation in this country has been engaged in its wars, and to Mr. Nanny is due the organization of the Orange County Chapter, of the Sons of the Revolution. His father Capt. Abram L. Nanny was well known during the days of the Civil War, as the Provost Marshal of the then 11th District, composed of the counties of Orange and Sullivan, under whose direction an enrollment of those liable to military duty, and a draft of 2,000 men therefrom, was made at Goshen, during a period of fierce political excitement, in 1863, at which time he was sustained by the 5th Regiment of Wisconsin and the 2d Connecticut Battery.

It was Mr. Nanny's desire to enter the Military Academy at West Point, but an affliction which resulted in permanent infirmity intervened on the eve of his appointment, and the would-be soldier was sent to College and reluctantly turned to another pursuit.

James M. Walker.

JAMES M., son of Jacob Walker and Mary C. Durkee, was born at Walker Valley, Ulster Co., February 28, 1845. He was educated in the public schools and completed a course of training in the Newburgh Business College. He assisted his father in all his business interests, in the store, on the farm, at the saw-mill and in all kinds of lumbering. In 1865 he took charge of the market wagon route from Walker Valley to Newburgh, selling farm produce and shipping butter to New York by way of Wm. K. Mailler's barge. In 1868 and '69, he filled the same position for Mr. C. Barnhart, to whom his father had sold the store and business in Walker Valley. In 1870 his father built the three-story brick building on Montgomery Street, Walden, and on May 9th of that year it was opened for business under the firm name of Jacob Walker & Son. In 1877 they enlarged the building, and in 1880, Jacob Walker, the senior member of the firm retired and James S. Eaton took his place, and the firm of Walker & Eaton was formed. Again the building was enlarged and the drug department added. They bought the grocery stock from A. S. Tears and from Hiram B. Wooster in 1885, and conducted two stores until February 1st, 1894, when the firm was dissolved by mutual consent, J. M. Walker remaining at the old stand on Montgomery Street. The same year he adopted the cash system and now finds it necessary to enlarge his space.

He was a member of the board of village trustees for a period of about five years. He has been an officer in the Walden M. E. Church twenty-five years, was president of the board of trustees and superintendent of the Sabbath School for about five years. He has also been a trustee of the Wallkill Valley Church for the past ten years. He has never engaged to any extent in matters pertaining to politics, but his influence has always been thrown in the temperance side of the question at issue.

Whitfield Gibbs.

WHITFIELD GIBBS was born at Hope, N. J., January 28, 1851. He is a son of Levi B. and the late Ellen Vanatta Gibbs. He was given a common school education in his native village. The first four years of his business career was spent clerking in a store. He then went to Newton, N. J., where he learned the printing business in the office of the *Sussex Register*, and later worked at his trade in Newark and New York. In 1878, with I. J. Stanton, he purchased the *Deckertown Independent*, and after conducting that for four years, he disposed of his interest to his partner. He afterwards held the position of city editor of the *Jersey City Daily Argus*, and also editor of the *Passaic Daily Times*. Previous to purchasing *The Walden Citizen*, he was Purchasing Agent of the Pennsylvania, Poughkeepsie and Boston R. R. In July, 1898, he purchased *The Walden Citizen*, which was then a folio, but he at once converted it into a quarto, which is a live local weekly newspaper.

Alexander Kidd.

ALEXANDER KIDD was born at St. Andrews, a beautiful hamlet in the town of Montgomery, N. Y. (The historical events of its past have been graphically described by one of its residents on page twenty-four of this volume). Mr. Kidd's parents were Lotan Kidd and Eliza Woodruff, honored citizens of their day and generation. Early in life he inclined to an active life, and during years spent at Newburgh, N. Y., he served as a member of the old Cataract Engine Company, No. 3, and was also a member of the Washington Continental Guards under Captain Isaac Wood, receiving an honorable discharge; he served full time in the Nineteenth Regiment of Orange County under Captain Peter Latourette. Later Mr. Kidd enlisted in the Fifty-sixth N. Y. S. V. under Colodel C. H. Van Wyck. At the expiration of two years, on account of illness contracted, he was honorably discharged at Seabrook, S. C. In 1866 he began a general grocery business at Newburgh, N. Y., under the firm name of A. & T. Kidd. In 1875 he removed to Orange Lake, Orange County, N. Y., and conducted a hotel, and in 1880, at the same place, opened the Lake Side House, at that time a noted resort for summer tourists. During his management of seven years a very large and prosperous business was established. In 1887 Mr. Kidd removed to Walden, N. Y., and has since conducted a large and modern hotel. At St. Andrew's is a large tract of fertile land known as the "Old Kidd Homestead," which has been in possession of the Kidd family since early in the seventeenth century; recently it passed to the ownership of the subject of this sketch, who bears the name of his honored grandfather. In 1865 Mr. Kidd was married to Miss C. B. Smith, of Montgomery, N. Y. Their only child, Lewis W., resides at Walden, N. Y.

In Memoriam,

OR THE

RECOGNITION OF FRIENDS BEYOND THE LIMITATIONS OF THIS LIFE.

"We are quite sure
That He will give them back,
Bright, pure and beautiful.
We know He will but keep
Our own and His, until we fall asleep.
We know He does not mean
To break the strands reaching between
Me here and there.
He does not mean though Heaven be fair
To change spirits entering there,
That they forget the eyes upraised and wet,
The lips too still for prayer,
The mute despair.
He will not take
The spirits which He gave, and make
The glorified so new,
That they are lost to me and you,
I do believe
They will receive
Us—you and me—and be so glad
To meet us, that when most I would grow sad,
I just begin to think about the gladness
And the day,
When they shall tell us all about the way
That they had learned to go,
Heaven's pathway show.
My lost, my own and I,
Shall have so much to see together by and by,
I do believe that just the same sweet face
But glorified, is waiting in the place
Where we shall meet if only I
Am counted worthy in that by and by,
I do believe that God will give a sweet surprise
To tear-stained, saddened eyes,
And that His heaven will be
Most glad, with joy for you and me,
As we have suffered most.
God never made
Spirit for spirit answering shade for shade,
And placed them side by side,
So wrought in one, though separate, mystified
And meant to break,
The quivering threads between.
When we shall wake
I am quite sure we shall be very glad
That for a little while we were so sad."

In Memoriam.

John Gail Borden.

JOHN GAIL BORDEN was born in Galveston, Texas, January 4, 1844. He was the youngest son of that great public benefactor, Gail Borden. Coming north with his father when but a lad of thirteen he attended one of the public schools of Brooklyn for a time, and from there went to Winchester Center, Conn., where he entered the Winchester Academy. From Winchester a business college was the next step in his educational course, but this was interrupted by the Civil war; for, like many of "Our Boys" in the recent Spanish-American war, he left the school room in response to his country's call for volunteers. He enlisted in the 150th New York Volunteers and served under Colonel (later General) John Henry Ketcham for two years and a half, during which time he worked his way to the rank of SecondLieutenant. The long, continued active service and exposure brought on an illness, compelling retirement from the army for several months, when he recovered sufficiently to again resume his duties, and was transferred to the Forty-seventh New York Volunteers, with which regiment he remained until the close of the war, participating with it in the Florida campaign. Returning to his home in Brewster, N. Y., when mustered out of service, Mr. Borden became identified with the New York Condensed Milk Company, where his inventive genius and energy played a conspicuous part in the perfecting of his father's inventions. Later he was elected president of the company and filled this position most successfully until 1885. In 1881 Mr. Borden moved from Brewster to Wallkill, Ulster County, where he built the condensery for the N. Y. C. M. Co., at the same time beginning on an extensive scale the farming operations which have made the Borden's Home Farm one of the model practical farms of this State. Failing health in 1885 compelled retirement from an active business life, when he turned his whole attention toward improving and beautifying his farm, trying, as he often expressed it, "to make two blades of grass grow where but one grew before." How well he succeeded has been demonstrated by the bountiful crops gathered from year to year on the "Home Farm." Mr. Borden's intense patriotism led him to become one, if not the first, of the pioneers in the work of inculcating a love of country and the "Stars and Stripes" in the hearts of the children, and to this end made a practice on Decoration Days of presenting each child in the public schools in his vicinity, both North and South, a small American flag, as he felt the future of our country rested with the rising generation. Devotion to home and country were among Mr. Borden's strong characteristics. The good he accomplished in his forty-seven years of life cannot be recorded here. He left an enviable record—that of an energetic, Christian gentleman who devoted his time, talents, and means to the uplifting of humanity. Mr. Borden died in October, 1891, at his winter home in Ormond, Fla. We close this brief sketch with a quotation from an obituary taken from *The Coast Gazette*, an Ormond paper:—

"Thus have we lost a good friend in common with all the State; a man of kindly heart, intelligent and far seeing, he used his wealth to benefit others far more than himself individually, and wherever he tarried, whether amongst the green hills of the North, by the waters of the St. Johns, on the shores of the Halifax, or amid the sand dunes of the beach, his hand and genius were ever busy to beautify and improve as well as to stimulate and help others. More capable hands will write his biography, which, when done as it deserves to be, will show forth a noble example, to be esteemed and followed by others upon whom Providence has showered wealth."

History of "Home Farm."

The Wallkill is the western boundary of the "Home Farm;" its southern limit is the land owned by the New York Condensed Milk Company, while on the east and north lie the various farms once forming the northeastern tract deeded by good Queen Anne. In the year 1750 a part of this royal grant passed into the possession of a Hasbrouck, and was inherited and held by the Hasbrouck heirs until the years 1866 and 1872, at which dates certain portions of said parcel of land, called "Lot No. 6," passed into the possession of Mr. John P. Andrews. This gentleman maintained the property as a farm and summer residence, carefully preserving the old stone house built by the Hasbroucks in 1771. During Mr. Andrews' ownership many improvements were made and an addition built to the old homestead. In the year 1881 the "Andrews' Farm" passed into the possession of John G. Borden, who began immediately to acquire the smaller farms adjoining him, until they came to form a part of the present "Home Farm," the name given it by Mr. Borden. The natural attractions of "Home Farm" are too familiar to the readers of the Souvenir to need description here. It was not our design, in this brief sketch, to describe its many attractions or to sound the praises of the one who devoted the last ten years of his life to its development, and who now sleeps amidst the daily routine of its busy life.

In Memoriam.

Robert Young.

ROBERT YOUNG was born in the town of Montgomery, N. Y., November 28, 1818, being the eldest son of Johnston and Margaret Barkley Young. He received his education at the Montgomery Academy, where he was preparing to enter college, but owing to the death of his father it became necessary for him to devote his time to agricultural pursuits. He was a man intellectually far above the average of his fellows, was well read, possessed an excellent memory, independent in his thought and action, always doing his own thinking and giving out his opinion without fear or favor. Mr. Young was fond of controversy and debate and many years ago when debating societies were in vogue he was always present at the Goodwill schoolhouse and was the life of the society. In 1879 he was elected supervisor of the town of Montgomery, which office he held eight consecutive years, from 1879 to 1886, and again for one year in 1890, which was his last public service, being an efficient member of the board, and looked well after the interests of the town. At the time of his death, in September, 1895, he held the office of district clerk, having filled that office for fifty-four years. In May, 1862, he married Miss Emily Crawford Arnott, who, with four children, survive him, their son Robert Jr.'s death preceding his father's by two years, and a daughter, Eliza Crawford, who died in infancy.

In Memoriam.

Floyd H. Reevs.

FLOYD H. REEVS was born in Westtown, Orange County, New York, December 29, 1837. He was a son of Charles W. and Azubah Lee Reevs. At the age of ten years he moved with his father's family to Goshen. Received his education at Charlottesville, N. Y. At an early age he became a partner with his father in the mercantile business under the firm C. W. Reevs & Son; his father died September 2, 1865. March 1, 18[illegible], the partnership of Reevs & Kelsey was formed, which relation continued until his death, March 4, 1898. He was a man of independent thought and action, possessed a natural inquiring mind and always completed whatever he undertook when he had once in his mind the object worthy of his support. He was an honest, upright business man. He was vice-president of the Goshen Savings Bank, and in all matters which have tended in the line of Goshen's prosperity he was progressive. In religious matters he has been prominent all his life. Had he not been a successful man of business he would have been a successful preacher, for he was an eloquent and effective speaker in religious gatherings, and in the great revival in Goshen Methodist Church in the early seventies his earnest and powerful addresses will long be remembered. In 1863 he married Christine, daughter of John and Hannah DeKay Cowdrey. To them was born two daughters, Mrs. Wilmot Makuen and Miss Clara. He was buried from his late residence; interment, Slate Hill Cemetery, Goshen, New York.

In Memoriam.

Chancy Hulse.

CHANCY HULSE was born in Blooming Grove, this county, May 2, 1827. He was a son of Meads T. and Dollie (Stewart) Hulse. He was reared on his father's farm, and after securing a fair education began to clerk in a store at Burnside. At the age of seventeen he was apprenticed to learn the trade of a watch case manufacturer with Charles Hulse, at which he served four years and a half, then secured a position in New York City, where he remained for ten years. He then settled in Washingtonville, Orange County, where he manufactured watch cases until 1866. The following year he came to Goshen, where he purchased a jewelry business, and from that time forward success crowned his efforts. During the last fifteen years of his life the business was conducted under the firm name of C. Hulse & Son. In 1884, together with his son, L. W., they began dealing in wagons and carriages under the style of the Hulse Wagon Company. Politically he was a staunch Republican, and for several terms he served as Trustee of the Village Board. He was enterprising and public spirited, and it was due to his influence and progressive spirit, in a great measure, that Goshen attained its present prosperity. His first wife was Susan Jane, daughter of George and Susan (Cooley) McKinney, natives of Orange County. To them were born two children, a son, Lewis W., and a daughter, Susie. The mother of these children died in 1865, and for his second wife he married Frances C., daughter of Hudson Webb, of Hamptonburgh. He died May 20, 1895, and was buried from the Presbyterian Church, of Goshen; interment at Slate Hill Cemetery.

In Memoriam.

John S. Taylor.

MR. TAYLOR was born in Warwick, N. Y., December 6, 1832, was a son of Isaac and Margaret (Smith) Taylor, the former a native of Sussex County, N. J., and the latter of Warwick, N. Y. John S. Taylor remained with his parents until the age of twenty five when he was married and for ten years operated the old farm of two hundred and forty acres which he then owned. At the end of that period he came to Walden and started the [illegible] and [illegible] business. He never took active part in political matters and was not bound by party ties, [illegible] to vote for the man best qualified to fill the office, regardless of the party to which he belonged. He was ever interested in the welfare of the community. He served as President of the Walden Knife Co. [illegible] President and Trustee of the village ten years, President and Trustee of the village school two [illegible] and President of the water works three years. Mr. Taylor was twice married, his first union being with Miss Mary W. Brooks of Warwick, who died April 30, 1886, leaving two sons, Newton [illegible] of Walden. On the 16th of November, 1887, Mr. Taylor was married to Mrs. [illegible] Edward Whitehead, President of the Walden Knife Company. On the morning of Jan. [illegible] the limitations of this present life, and on Feb. 3rd his interment was made at the Wallkill Valley Cemetery, Walden, N. Y.

In Memoriam.

M. Gedney Snyder.

M. GEDNEY SNYDER was born on the ancestral homestead near Orange Lake in the town of Newburgh, N.Y., August 7, 1833. Mr. Snyder's early life inclined to agriculture and he became one of the representative farmers of Orange county. In 1861 he married Mrs. C. Louise Gedney of New York city. Mr. and Mrs. Snyder selected for their home a large and pleasantly located farm at St. Andrews, N. Y. As the years passed extensive improvements were made, the land brought to a high state of cultivation, the buildings modernized and enlarged, making a beautiful suburban home. Mr. Snyder was known as a thrifty and successful farmer, whose well cultivated domain and attractive surroundings were evidence of his enterprise and prosperity. For a long series of years he was trustee of the public school and at the time of his death in 1895 was a director of the Walden National bank, which position he had filled for many years, greatly to the financial interests of that institution. He was laid at rest in the family plot in the Wallkill Valley cemetery at Walden.

In Memoriam.

Nicholas I. Quackenbos.

NICHOLAS I. QUACKENBOS, the subject of this sketch, descended from an old and honored New York family. He was born in the city of New York, April 11, 1838. His parents were Mangle Minthorne and Julia (Clark) Quackenbos. When about twenty-one years of age Mr. Quackenbos selected Montgomery, N. Y., as his future place of residence, where he purchased a tract of land very pleasantly situated, which he brought to a high state of cultivation and later erected thereon one of the most modern homes in the valley of the Wallkill. Mr. Quackenbos was [illegible] strong [illegible] characteristics, blended with many graces. Throughout his life his family and home were [illegible] his deepest [illegible] and his highest ambition. He gave liberally of his wealth to the support of his Church [illegible]. He had the happy faculty of forming close, true friendships, with a magnetic power that drew to him [illegible] the hearts of those with whom he came in touch. He died at his residence at Montgomery, Wednesday, November 23, 1898; interment was at Brick Church Cemetery, Montgomery, N. Y.

In Memoriam.

Daniel Millspaugh Wade.

DANIEL MILLSPAUGH WADE was born at Montgomery, N. Y., December 16, 1832. The boyhood days of Mr. Wade were passed in Montgomery. Early in life he learned the tinsmith's trade and soon established a business of his own, continuing it until August, 1891, making thirty-nine years of continuous business in the same locality. On the 26th of March, 1856, a wedding ceremony was performed which united the destinies of Mr. Wade and Miss Charlotte C. David, a daughter of Daniel and Elizabeth (Constable) David. Mr. Wade was always an active worker in the Presbyterian Church, in which he served as elder for fifteen years. He was most earnest in his support of all work tending to improve and elevate the kindred interests of his town and county. In early life he was a Democrat; later he gave his allegiance to the Prohibition party. For three years he represented his town as supervisor, also served as a member of the School Board, of which he was president for some years. Mr. Wade was also a trustee of his native village. His genial manners and sturdy integrity won him hosts of friends, who held him in high esteem. Mr. Wade accumulated a competency, retiring from business several years before his death, which occurred at Montgomery in January, 1899. His interment was at the Presbyterian Cemetery, Montgomery, N. Y.

In Memoriam.

Rev. Martin V. Schoonmaker, D. D.

REV. MARTIN V. SCHOONMAKER, D. D., died at Allenhurst, N. J., June 16, 1899, aged 82 years. [illegible]

[illegible] with his [illegible] articles, "Recollections of a Pastorate," and "[illegible] Souvenirs for 1895 and 1896, respectively, are remembered by the readers [illegible]

In Memoriam.

John Mould.

THE subject of this sketch was born in 1813. He came from a family whose representatives were numbered among the earliest settlers of the Valley of the Wallkill, the remote ancestors being natives of Holland. Mr. Mould was born in the town of Montgomery, N. Y., and spent his entire life of nearly seventy-six years upon the farm on which he was born. He was well known as one of the energetic and successful citizens of the locality. Mr. Mould was a strong Republican, an earnest and active member of the old Brick (Reformed) Church. For a long series of years he served as elder, and at his death was the senior elder of his Church. Mr. Mould married Miss Emily Douglas, who was almost a life-long member of the Brick Church. The interment of John and Emily Mould was at the Brick Church Cemetery, Montgomery, N. Y.

In Memoriam.

J. Edward Baker.

J. EDWARD BAKER, who, for a number of years prior to his death was one of the influential business men of Newburgh, was born near Buffalo, N. Y., being a son of Michael H. and Amelia (Shay) Baker, the former [illegible], a native of Germany, and the latter of Erie County, N. Y. In Newburgh, where his boyhood days were passed, he was educated in Professor Brown's private school. He had a natural talent for stone lettering, and afterward worked at that business for several years. At the suggestion of his father a partnership was formed between the two and they embarked in the manufacture of mineral waters. This connection continued until the death of his father in 1885, when the son succeeded to the business and continued until his death November [illegible]. He was liberal to all churches and charitable enterprises, and it may with truth be said of him that his was an honest, upright and moral life. The lady who was Mr. Baker's faithful helpmate in life bore the maiden name of Rosa Viola Ramsperger. On the death of her husband she succeeded to the management of the business, which she has since carried on.

MONUMENT ERECTED IN OLD TOWN BURYING GROUND.

Near the corner of Liberty and South Streets, Newburgh, New York, by Quassaick Chapter, Daughters of the American Revolution, to Mark the Site of the First Church in Newburgh. Unveiled May [illegible]

Sunshine and Shadow of a Farmer's Life.

CHARLES RIVENBURG.

NEVER having been a farmer, it may seem to you like presumption on my part to speak on the subject assigned me, "Sunshine and Shadow of a Farmer's Life;" and yet, may it not be possible from the vantage ground of a non-personally interested observer, to see some things more clearly than can be realized by those hampered by familiarity of occupation.

This is the age when we are delighted to boast of antiquity in architecture, in furniture, in family, in jewels and ornaments, in art, in sculpture, in occupation. How proud we are to point to the age of our business houses; how for generations in the past our ancestors have followed the same line. However, we must all give the palm for antiquity to the agriculturist. Your ancestral estate was the garden of Eden. Adam was the first husbandman as well as the first husband; Eve, the first milkmaid. Think of the delicious richness of that snowy fluid in those days. No microbes, no chalk, no salt, no water needed, no leaky or stolen cans, no inspectors. In the course of time as year followed year, cycle after cycle, century after century, the only records with which both profane and sacred history have to do were with the tillers of the soil, and the raisers of flocks and herds. You farmers may therefore boast of your antiquity, for you reach back even to the laying of the corner-stone of the foundation of the world. You may boast of men in your occupation whose history after the lapse of thousands of years is common to every household wherever the sacred scriptures are read, and will so continue until the end of time. Men noted for character, probity, steadfastness of purpose, honored by God as well as man in all generations. How responsible, then, your occupation to sustain the dignity of manhood set by your progenitors. In this you will be sustained by the sunshine of worthy example.

SPRING BROOK, EAST WALDEN, N. Y.

Men engaged in the pursuits of learned professions and business life have cares, worries, trials and crosses of which the farmer by his genial fireside does not even dream. How frequently we hear sympathy expressed

WANTED

500 Men in the Wallkill Valley

To ship all their fruit this season via the **Poughkeepsie Bridge Road.** We offer you the best service in reaching all markets—New York, Jersey City, Paterson, Newark, Philadelphia, Hartford, Springfield, Providence, Worcester, Boston, etc. **We guarantee the continuance of rates and time and the prompt adjustment of any claims.** Get started right this year by shipping with us, thereby obtaining the lowest rates and early markets, also the best prices.

L. JOHNSTON, Agent, Highland, N. Y.
W. P. BISHOP, Agent, Loyd, N. Y.
W. T. REID, Agent, Clintondale, N. Y.
N. H. YEAGER, Agent, Modena, N. Y.

W. [illegible] MARTIN, Gen'l Freight Agent, Hartford, Conn.

A PARTIAL VIEW OF THE ARTIFICIAL LAKE IN THE RURAL GROUNDS, NEW JERSEY, ILLUSTRATIVE OF WHAT MAY BE ACCOMPLISHED TO ADORN AND BEAUTIFY SUBURBAN HOMES.

for the physician, who, when the thermometer reaches zero, in the face of a blinding storm of sleet, has to travel miles alone through the darkness of the night to visit the sick, while the farmer is peacefully sleeping. How often the lawyer who holds in his hands the keys of destiny for the prisoner on trial, whose offense is punishable with death, spends days and even weeks in the preparation and trial of the cause without rest or recreation, troubled with the demon of insomnia from nervousness, of exhaustion and grave responsibility. The statesman with the multitudinous cares of a nation dependent upon his skill and judgment in the formation of domestic measures, and in the comity of international affairs; the business man with notes coming due, with a small bank account and a large list of debtors who can not find it convenient to settle, suffer agonies with which the farmer is not on speaking acquaintance. Sunshine for the farmer is freedom from solicitude; shadows for all others.

All occupations and avocations other than that of husbandry, depend more or less upon public opinion. Even those who stand most high in the professional world must submit and cater to a great degree to the sentiment of the people. Their position in life, the financial success of men of affairs depends largely upon the impress they create upon the masses with whom they come in contact. The success of a salesman, and his promotions are determined by his apparent sweetness of disposition under any and all circumstances of annoyances. The farmer in the enjoyment of his broad acres, feels a kingly power. In these possessions he feels

Central-Hudson Steamboat Co.'s

.....DAILY LINES.....

NEWBURGH LINE.

Steamers Homer Ramsdell and Newburgh between New York and Newburgh.

LANDING AT

Rates of Fare.

POUGHKEEPSIE LINE.

Steamers D. S. Miller and J. L. Hasbrouck, between New York and Poughkeepsie.

LANDING AT

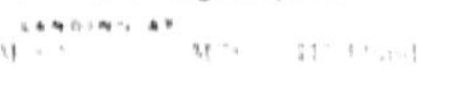

Rates of Fare.

KINGSTON LINE.

Steamers Wm. F. Romer and Jas. W. Baldwin, between New York and Kingston.

LANDING AT

West Point, Newburgh, New Hamburgh, Marlborough, Milton, Poughkeepsie, Esopus.

Leave Kingston daily, except Saturdays, 6:00 p. m. Leave New York foot West 10th St., week days, except Saturdays, 4:00 p. m.; Saturdays 1:00 p. m. Down Boat does not land at West Point.

Rates of Fare.

Between Kingston (Rondout), Esopus, and New York, one way, 75 cents; excursion, $1.25. Poughkeepsie, Milton, Marlborough, New Hamburgh and New York, one way, 60 cents; excursion, $1.00.

NEWBURGH & ALBANY LINE.

Between Newburgh and Albany, Stopping at Intermediate Landings.

Leaving Newburgh daily, except Sundays, at a. m. Leave Albany daily, except Sundays, a. m.

These Steamers extend their trips to Troy Mondays, Tuesdays, Thursdays and Fridays.

The Most Economical and Pleasant Way for Passenger Travel. Prompt Freight Service and Low Rates.

that none may chide, criticise, reprimand or deny, for of what avail would be any criticism. His products supply the human race. All things that make our world the paradise it is, must emanate from the soil; and the producer of wares for public necessity, is in a position of independence sweet to the human soul. Should business or pleasure call him away, he need not feel that clients or customers will seek other offices or stores in his absence. His fields will patiently await his return. Should illness or indisposition be his lot, his convalesence is materially aided by a quiet and submissive mind, whereas the man of business is laboring under a mighty strain for a quick recovery, and to that extent is handicapped by this anxiety to return to his office or behind his counter. Delightful then is the sunshine of the farmer's life.

PICTURESQUE DRIVES, LAKE MOHONK.

As we look over the toilers of this work-a-day world of ours, how many thousands of them we find shut up in hives of industry from early morn till darkness again spreads her mantle over the land, deprived of light and the sweet air of God's creation; numbers with pale and haggard countenances thirsting for the sunshine of healthfulness, imprisoned in musty offices or dingy counting rooms, and then that numerous class delving in the bowels of the earth so deep that there, light may not send her faintest pencil, thus living on a mere existence year after year, until the fell destroyer consigns them to mother earth, with whom from earliest childhood they were literally familiar. We now again direct our attention to the tiller of the soil. Do we see there the discontented expression, the slavish demeanor, the cadaverous face, the pale brow, the sunken eye, the emaciated form. No; sunshine, literally and figuratively, gives us a race well preserved and robust in appearance, with ruddy cheeks, happy and contented. Verily, the farmer's wife, and sons and daughters, all bespeak a life of sunshine, healthfulness and good appetites.

There seems some inherent quality indigenous to the soil for the creation of great men. Statistics and biographies teach us that the men who have moved the world as statesmen, inventors, promoters of the weal of the human race, were propogated on the farm. There were planted the strong physique, the personal force, the indomitable will that later make the world richer, purer and better, for the grand achievements made possible by drinking in through early years the sunshine and health giving ozone of a *free* country life.

'Tis true that a farmer's life will not produce for him great wealth. Should he continue this occupation during the term of his natural existence, his name will not descend to posterity as a great capitalist, the employer of thousands of men, the organizer of trusts, that giant octopus, sapping the life's blood of more honorable, yet, from the world's standpoint, less fortunate men; millions will not be his, but what will millions avail Dives as he stands before the great white throne. There we shall be known for our true worth, and stocks and bonds will not be at a premium on the judgment morn. Nevertheless, the occupation of farming should and does provide a competence for you in your old age, so that you may continue the journey of life to the final harbor with smooth seas. Life is not all the amassing of colossal fortunes, but it is so living that we may obtain from it the greatest good for ourselves and for our neighbors; the greatest joy and pleasure, with the least amount of care and annoyance. This is life as it should be lived.

MOUNTAIN ROADS, LAKE MOHONK.

What a perfect condition of joy to commune with nature under her most favorable conditions. To arise on a June morning to meet a greeting from an orchestra mighty in numbers, caroling music so sweet that angels might envy, refreshing one's eyes with the earth clothed in her magnificent beauty, the sparkling dew drops kissing one another, and anon scintillating like diamonds in a back ground of velvety green. Every where our gaze strays, new beauties burst upon us. The sun appearing over the eastern horizon, paints the fleecy clouds in

PICTURESQUE LAKE MOHONK.

brilliant colors and sends his beams across a sky of azure blue, thence shortly to steal down to fragrant flowers waiting in all their pristine purity for this morning salutation. What invigorating influences for the day of toil, with nature to cheer us with all her loveliness, and nature's God in our hearts creating a love for the beautiful; toil under these circumstances becomes a blessing, and when the evening comes with her restfulness, sweet contentment still reigns. Another picture of delight opens before us as the beautiful twilight colors light up the western sky. The gentle lowing of the cattle creates a soothing influence that lulls to slumber the weary yet happy husbandman.

Thus pass the days through seed time and harvest, each bringing sweetened toil and recreation, until barns, granaries and storehouses are bursting with the accumulations of golden grains supplied by a bountiful providence. Autumn soon appears with her artist brush and palette, decking hill and dale with a harmony of color never rivaled in the artificial landscape.

No pen, or brush can portray, no poet, be he ever so divine, can measure the depths of emotion aroused within our souls by the consciousness of the beautiful, by the realization that the Creator of this marvelous blending of lights and shades, of the combination of effects of orange and yellow, of blue and vermilion, is our God, educating us so that the home beyond the skies on our arrival there, shall not overwhelm us with its effulgence.

To the dwellers in city or town, flats or apartments, the home life of a farmer would be a revelation. Hemmed in by brick walls and stone pavements, human nature demands excitement. Interests aside from the

JOHNSTON & PECK

PRINTED THIS BOOK

47 49 and 51 Third Street
NEWBURGH NEW YORK

Consult Them

.....Do You Use Paper Boxes?

We are Manufacturers of all Kinds of Plain and Fancy

.....Paper Boxes.....

WE ARE WHOLESALE AND RETAIL DEALERS IN ALL KINDS OF

Wrapping Paper,
Paper Bags
and Twine

We are General Agents for The National Gum and Mica Co., Manufacturers of Pastes, Sizings and Liquid Glue

WRITE US

Newburgh Paper Box Factory,

F. WM. WENZEL, PROPRIETOR. 87 WATER STREET, NEWBURGH, N. Y.

WESLEY GROVE—THE OLD NEELEYTOWN CAMP MEETING GROUNDS, PHOTOGRAPHED SEPT. 1868.

family circle fill the mind. Children, almost, need introductions to fathers who are never seen at the family table during the day. Evenings are spent at the club or opera. Around the farmer's board the family life is made prominent. Community of interests makes the members thereof one kin, as strong as that of blood relationship. Here home life is at its acme of perfection. Love holds sway, each striving in the little family circle to center the delights of the whole world. Books, papers, periodicals and magazines read aloud by the father, while the mother with her work basket and her children gathered about her, form a picture of perfect contentment unknown to town life. Truly sunshine mellows the farmer's life.

As to the second part of my subject—the shadows, the corollary—I fail to find them. Sunshine presupposes shadows, as a natural sequence they should follow. Before I began to write, I wondered if my thoughts would not stray almost entirely amongst the shadows, but after some meditation, I found my fears groundless. As I traveled along I looked for the darkness—looked to the north, sunshine and pleasant warmth met me there; looked to the east, no shadow, nothing but brightness there; looking to the south, sunshine with gentle zephyrs, greet me there; looking to the west, still we bask in pleasant beams, not even fearing the coming night.

What the People Say:

THE LUDWIG PIANO CO. Here we
keep Pianos and Organs at prices cheaP

Leading instruments they supply
that cannot be surpassed say I

Unequalled for tone and touch, 'tis clear
to give satisfaction is their ideA

Durability and quality in them we gain
and utmost sweetness we obtain N

Well selected sheet music they will show
instrumental and vocal whene'er we gO

In Brass and String goods all agree
a fine selection here we C

Guaranteeing our tuning, repairing and
prices low, all favor the Ludwig Piano CO

57 Broadway and
16 Colden St.,

NEWBURGH, NEW YORK.

W. F. CONKLING
MANAGER.

.....The Greatest Charm

of any Piano is a sympathetic tone. Volumes of sound may be appreciated by some players, but the true music-lover has an ear only for the quality of tone. Our Pianos are constructed to give forth melody rather than to make noise. The music that is in them is identical in each instrument, the varied prices being graded according to cost of Cases.

Over Four Hundred of these Pianos

Sold in this vicinity. The only Piano sold that the maker has confidence enough in to

GUARANTEE
FOR A
LIFETIME.

Sunshine and Shadows of a Farmer's Life.

(CONCLUSION.)

Love, peace and repose—the tenderest trio
  Of musical words ever blended in one.
That one word is home—near the brook by the meadow
  Dear home of my childhood in years that are gone.

In fancy I wander on a sweet summer morning,
  Away to the wheat field just over the hill.
'Tis harvest time now, and the reapers are coming
  To gather the waiting grain, yellow and still.

Many harvests have passed, many summers have ended,
  Since here I oft toiled with glad reapers before,
And felt the great bounty of heaven extended
  Giving joy to the worker and bread to the poor.

Long ago I remember when thirsty and tiring
  The harvesters came to the old maple shade.
How they quaffed the pure water so cool and inspiring,
  That gushed from the fountain that nature had made.

And I think of the orchard, the apples that yellowed,
  Half hidden by leaves in the big early tree;
Ah, those apples how lucious, when ripened and mellowed,
  Then dropped in the clover for sister and me.

Old home of my youth, so humble and cherished,
  The hallow-ed memory cheers me to-day,
When all other thoughts of the past shall have perished,
  Remembrance of thee shall illumine the way.

Sweet home by the woodland, now farewell forever;
  I've wandered afar from thy dear cottage door.
I love thee, my farm home but never, no never,
  Thy sunshine and shadow shall cover me more.

AN OLD ELM, ULSTER COUNTY, N. Y.

It Will Pay You to Look at Our Stock

Shannon

& Co.,

SLATE ROOFERS

The Largest Mantle
Fire-Place and Tile House
Along the Hudson River.

WILL NOT BE UNDERSOLD

ALSO ACENT FOR

Philadelphia and Boston Fire-Brick Mantel.

107 LIBERTY STREET, NEWBURGH, NEW YORK.

Wiley & Co., Cayuga, New York.

ESTABLISHED 1847.

FRUIT TREES

Constitutionally hardy. So made by carefully guarded parentage in propagation. A whole PEACH ORCHARD for $——, well enough to box and pack them all.

MERSEREAU BLACKBERRY

Fruited six years and has not developed a weak point Largest, Sweetest and Most Productive. A full line of well-bred Fruit Trees. CASH PREMIUMS WITH SEED POTATOES.

DEWEY POTATO

Worth a good deal to read about this to say nothing of eating it. One order for anything our catalogue names will make you A LIFE-LONG CUSTOMER.

REMEMBER WE ARE HEADQUARTERS FOR ALL KINDS OF FRUIT TREES AND SMALL FRUITS AND SEED POTATOES.

Historical--Orange County Sunday School Association.

WILLIAM C. HART.

THE mission of this publication would be remiss in its duty, if in connection with the churches of the Wallkill Valley, some mention were not made of the great work of the Sabbath Schools associated therewith. In city and village, in every sequestered hamlet, are men and women of the highest type of God's creation, whose hearts go out in sympathy with the salvation of child life; whose best efforts, whose influence, whose earnest prayers are for turning such lives to a realization of the life eternal. In one of God's acres, "Berea Cemetery," Montgomery, N. Y., may be found the grave of Joseph B. Lawson, a man of blessed memory, an earnest prayerful member of a Union Sunday School, at St. Andrews, N. Y., who taught a large class of boys through a series of years, and lived to see each one become a communicant of the church on earth.

It was the privilege of the writer to be numbered with this particular class, and now in humble gratitude records this tribute to his memory. While John R. Wiltsie of Newburgh had large business interests to engross his mind, at least, he was an earnest Christian man. Mr. Wiltsie long felt that the interests of Sunday Schools would receive a great impetus if those working on the same lines could meet together in convention. Consequently, notices were sent out, and a large number of those friendly to the cause assembled at the First Congregational Church, Middletown, N. Y., on May 22d, 1861, at 10 A. M., when the *first Orange County Sunday School Association* was organized, embracing all the towns of the county. The attendance was large, and the sessions inspiring. Among these early members we note Rev. J. Forsyth, Rev. G. H. Mandeville, John R. Wiltsie, Charles Estabrook, Rev. John Crane, Rev. D. N. Freeland; Rev. L. Littell, Mt. Hope; Rev. M. V. Schoonmaker, Walden; Rev. D. C. Niven, Westtown; Rev. R. H. Wallace, Little Britain; Rev. S. S. Mills, Deerpark; Rev. D. Maclise, Montgomery; Rev. J. B. Ten Eyck, Montgomery; Rev. J. Erskin, Montgomery; A. Denniston, Washingtonville; Richard Coldwell, Blooming Grove; H. Barnes, Crawford; W. E. Mapes, Howells; C. E. Millspaugh, Goshen; Wm. L. Fairchild, Walden; John Verity. Walden; Wm. E. Gowdy, Walden; A. W. Cook, Walden, Sidney Kidd, Walden; W. C. Hart, Walden; Dr. Crane, Goshen; Isaac Swift, Minisink; Charles Young, Hamptonburgh; G. B. Mapes, Greenville; C. Mills, Florida; David Coleman, Wallkill; Charles Knapp, Little Britain; Conard Laskamp, Coldenham; Joel T. Headley, New Windsor; James Mills, Hampton; Lewis M. Smith, James H. Phillips, H. S. Banks, John Martin, Newburgh.

THE OLD KIDD HOMESTEAD, ALEX. KIDD, OWNER, WALDEN, N. Y.

On October 8, the Society met at the Reformed Church, Newburgh, nearly every school in the county being represented. It was decided that the Society hold quarterly sessions. Our limited space will only permit of brief mention as we trace the work of the organization.

Reformed Church, Walden, April 29; Presbyterian Church, Middletown, July 15; October 4, 1862, Presbyterian Church, Cornwall. The county report gave 18 towns. Officers and teachers, 1,118; scholars, 6,808; average attendance, 4,973; conversions, 144. April 14, 1863, Presbyterian Church, Monroe; July 14, Baptist Church, Newburgh. The first collection $20, was here taken, for incidental expenses. Mr. Charles Estabrook was elected secretary, and as the years passed by was very active and useful in the Society's life. Mr. Estabrook was in great demand to address the children, and had the happy faculty of holding their closest attention, as well as all who came in touch with his impressive manner, when he addressed an audience. Mr. Estabrook now holds the position of City Librarian at Newburgh, which place he has filled for nearly 30 years. October 13, at Warwick Reformed Church, the president, Rev. L. P. Ledoux, exhibited a head of wheat grown from a grain of wheat found in the head of a mummy that had been entombed three thousand years ago. July 20, 1864, Presbyterian Church, Goshen, Rev. G. H. Mandeville, of Newburgh, elected president; October 25, M. E. Church, Middletown; April 25, 1865, M. E. Church, Port Jervis; July 25, Calvary Presbyterian Church, Newburgh, elected Thomas B. Scott, president, J. H. Phillips, secretary;

ESTABLISHED 1791

John R. McCullough,

(Successor to JOHN W. McCULLOUGH.)

ALL THE LEADING BRANDS OF TOBACCOS, CIGARETTES, IMPORTED KEY WEST AND DOMESTIC CIGARS.

Wholesale and Retail.

Dealers Will Find It to Their Advantage to Call, Inspect Goods and Get Prices.

YOUR TRADE SOLICITED.

68 Water Street, Newburgh, N. Y.

JOHN J. E. HARRISON,

(SUCCESSOR TO BROWN LIME CO.)

Broadway, Newburgh, N. Y.

The Best, Strongest and Cheapest Manufactured.

Rosendale Cement, Portland Cement, Fire Cement, Land Plaster, Building Plaster, White Sand, Marble Dust, Front Brick, Hard Brick, Fire Brick---all shapes; Bone Phosphate---pure; Dain Pipe---all sizes; Fittings---all shapes; Mortar Colors, Plastering Hair, etc., Rifle Powder, Blasting Powder, Fuse of All Kinds, Dynamite, and Caps for Same.

GOODS SHIPPED ON ELECTRIC RAILWAY. **Telephone, 144-D.**

MILK PRODUCERS OF THE WALLKILL VALLEY.

Mrs. J. Ed. Baker's

PREMIUM SUPERIOR
MINERAL WATERS.

FOR SALE BY ALL FIRST-CLASS DEALERS.

OFFICE AND FACTORY:
417 Washington St., Newburgh, N. Y.

J. HUMPHREY,

4 Water St.,
Newburgh, N. Y.

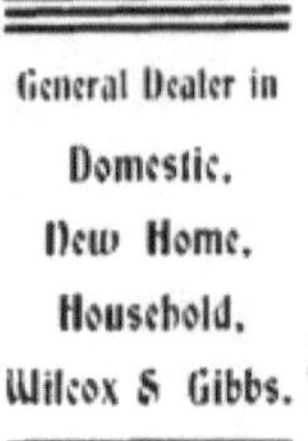

General Dealer in

Domestic,
New Home,
Household,
Wilcox & Gibbs.

MACHINES.

Needles and attachments for all Machines.
Machines Rented, Exchanged or Repaired.

. . . E. PINDAR . . .

Choice
Confectionery,

72 BROADWAY,
NEAR
GRAND ST.,
NEWBURGH,
NEW YORK.

Ice Cream,
...Fruits, etc...

FOR THE FIFTH SUCCESSIVE SEASON WILL BE ON THE GROUNDS OUTING DAY AND SUPPLY THE PEOPLE WITH THE ABOVE ARTICLES.

October 24, Presbyterian Church, Montgomery; April 24, 1866, M. E. Church, Washingtonville, special collection $115; July 24, Reformed Associate Church, Little Britain, Rev. R. Howard, elected president; vice presidents, T. B. Scott, Rev. J. M. McNulty; corresponding secretary, Hon. H. B. Bull, Montgomery; recording secretary, T. J. Bonnell, Port Jervis; October 30, M. E. Church, Port Jervis; April 30, Presbyterian Church, Middletown; August 6, 1867, 1st Presbyterian Church, Chester; October 29, 1867, Presbyterian Church, Canterbury; July, 1868, Presbyterian Church, Montgomery; April 28, Presbyterian Church, Cornwall Landing; April 28, First Presbyterian Church, Washingtonville, C. E. Millspaugh, of Goshen, was elected corresponding secretary. The reports from towns gave 102 schools; 1,496 teachers and officers; 8,879 scholars; 417 conversions—three towns not reporting. The brothers J. S. C. Abbott and Lyman Abbott were present, and gave great interest to the sessions. An incident was related of a teacher who taught a Bible Class of seventy (70), had been wonderfully blest by seeing sixty-nine (69) become communicants of Christian churches. October 4, First Presbyterian Church, Monroe. This session was memorable from the death record of active members of the Association. We note in full:

"The committee appointed at the last meeting of this Association to present a minute concerning the decease of Hon. Robert Denniston, Rev. Daniel Higbie, Rev. Jos. H. Robinson, Mr. John Jaques and Rev. Robt. H. Wallace, D. D., would most respectfully report the following for the adoption of this Association:

"Whereas, It has pleased Almighty God in the dispensation of His Providence to remove from us Hon. Robert Denniston, elder in the Presbyterian Church at Washingtonville, who for almost half a century had been identified with the Sabbath School cause in this county, Rev. Daniel Higbie the pastor, and Mr. John Jaques, the efficient superintendent of the Sabbath School attached to the same church, thus taking from it pastor, elder and superintendent in the space of a few months to enter upon, as we believe, the realization of their hopes; and whereas, our young brother, Rev. Joseph H. Robinson, pastor of the church at Cornwall Landing, has also been taken from our band of Sabbath School workers, at the very commencement of the Christian warfare, and whereas, also Rev. Robert H. Wallace, D. D., who in years gone by in the church of his fathers stood up for, and defended the rights of the children, to the blessings of the Gospel, against the prejudices and opinions of many of that day, has also fallen at a ripe old age, 'full of years and full of honor.'

"Therefore, we desire to enter upon record this, our humble tribute, to the faithfulness and labors of love of our departed brethren, and to express our gratitude to the great head of the church for permitting them to labor so faithfully and well in the Master's vineyard—setting us a precious example, and when at last, when their work was over, enabling them to triumph through the riches of divine grace. Whilst we sympathize with the relatives of our departed friends in their sad and severe bereavements, we rejoice that they sorrow not as those who have no hope, for we know that those who sleep in Jesus, will God bring with him to the enjoyment of a better life."

April 13, 1869, M. E. Church, Walden; August 10, morning session, M. E. Church,

E. A. BROWN & SON

RATES $2.00 PER DAY.

Headquarters for the Orange County Agricultural Society.

E. A. BROWN
O. H. BROWN

MIDDLETOWN, N. Y.

Newburgh and Haverstraw Line.

STEAMER EMELINE.

Captain D. C. Woolsey.

IF YOU HAVE HAY OR STRAW TO SELL, CALL AND GET PRICES.

P. O. ADDRESS:

Box 78, Newburgh. *Box 425, Haverstraw.*

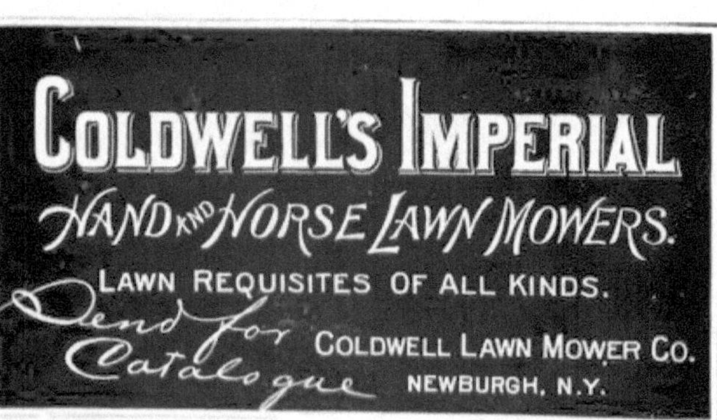

EVERY MACHINE WARRANTED.

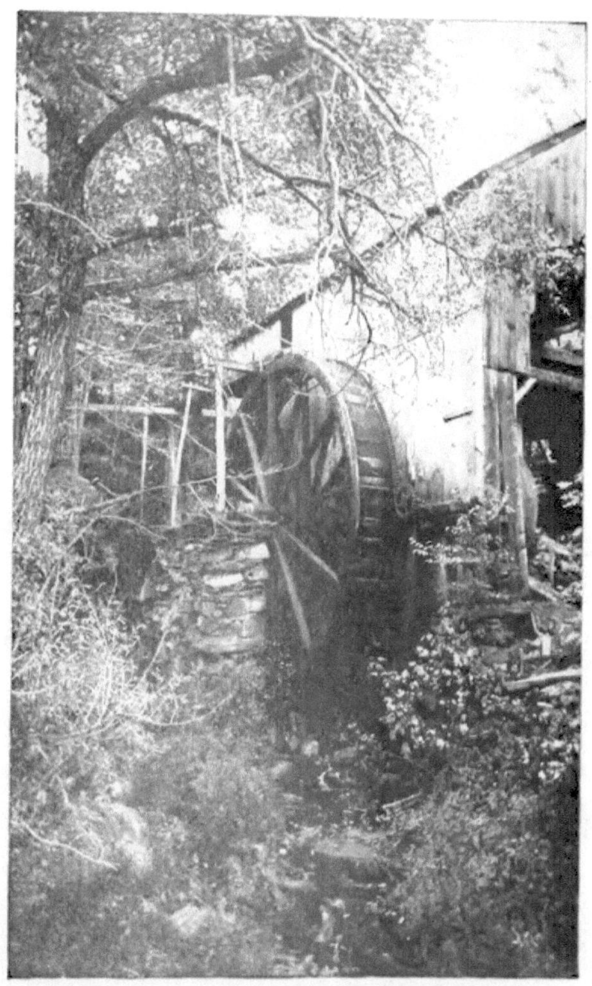

A MILL OF THE OLDEN TIMES, ULSTER COUNTY, N. Y.

afternoon session, Reformed Church, evening, Baptist Church, Port Jervis; the death of Hon. H. B. Bull, of Montgomery, was announced, and suitable resolutions passed. The following officers were elected: President, Rev. R. Howard Wallace, Little Britain; vice president, Charles Estabrook, Newburgh; secretary and treasurer, William C. Hart, Walden; May 18, 1870, Presbyterian Church, Florida; November 9, Union Church, Newburgh—large attendance; August 10, 1870, Congregational Church, Middletown, the birthplace of the Society, also witnessed the disbanding of the Association, and the re-organization of the present Society, under the same name. It was a grave error, and the only cause that led to the action, was to dispense with a cumbersome Constitution and By-laws, and adopt one brief in wording, yet amply covering all requisite conditions.

A special committee had labored long and earnestly to prepare a statistical report of the condition of the schools of the county, which was very ably presented by C. E. Millspaugh; 3,000 copies of this paper were printed and distributed. The afternoon session was so largely attended, that adjournment was made to a larger audience room, the Presbyterian Church edifice. The report of the treasurer for the year, showed receipts $207.64.

November 8 and 9, 1870, the first semi-annual convention convened at St. John's Church, Newburgh; May 31, 1871, at Warwick; June 5, 1872, Presbyterian Church, Goshen. Officers elected: President, Rev. Wendell Prime, Newburgh; vice president, Rev. C. A. Harvey, Middletown; secretary and treasurer, W. C. Hart, Walden. The latter tendered his resignation, and W. E. Mapes was elected to fill the vacancy; November 2, 1872, First Presbyterian Church, Middletown; May 13, 1879, Union Presbyterian Church, Newburgh. Officers elected: President, Rev. Jas. M. Dickson, Montgomery; secretary, Rev. A. H. Saxe, Walden; treasurer, James H. Phillips, Newburgh; June 16, 1880, Presbyterian Church, Goshen; 131 Sunday Schools; 2,011 officers and teachers; 10,175 children and youth; 2,648 adults; 16,598 total enrollment; conversions 396; contributions $5,714.24; May 31, 1881, 2d Presbyterian Church, Washingtonville; May 22, 1882, M. E. Church, Warwick; June 14, 1883, Presbyterian Church, Middletown: President, Arthur Jones, Newburgh; secretary, Floyd H. Crane, Goshen; treasurer, I. H. Jackson, Montgomery; May 13, 1884, 2d Presbyterian Church, Florida; May 12, 1885, Presbyterian Church, Chester; May 18, 1886, Presbyterian Church, Cornwall; May 10, 1887, Reformed Church, Port Jervis; May 15, 1888, Presbyterian Church, Goshen, Rev. W. S. Winans, Jr., Goshen, president; May 21, 1889, Moffatt Library, Washingtonville; May 20, 1890, Walden; May 20, 1891, Warwick, Richard Caldwell, Salisbury Mills, president; F. A. Crane, secretary; May 18, 1892, M. E. Church, Cornwall; president, Emmett A. Browne, Port Jervis; May 17, 1893, Presbyterian Church, Highland Falls, president, R. S. Talbot, Cornwall; secretary, A. B. Hurtin, Middletown; May 16, 1894, Montgomery, president, H. N. Greene, Washingtonville; May 15, 1895, Presbyterian Church, Port Jervis, president, C. E. Millspaugh, Goshen; secretary, O. B. Hurtin, Middletown; treasurer, C. A. Brown, Port Jervis; May 15, 1896, Presbyterian Church, Chester; May 12, 1897, Trinity Church, Newburgh; May 25, 1898, Reformed Church, Walden, president, E. C. Barnes, Newburgh; corresponding secretary, W. F.

PROMINENT COMMISSION HOUSE

ESTABLISHED 1865.

S. H. & E. H. Frost,

319 WASHINGTON
COR. JAY ST.,
NEW YORK.

Members of the National League of Commission Merchants of the United States. Leading Dealers in Fruits, Produce, Poultry. Dressed Calves a Specialty.

As a Rule, Brothers Work Well Together in Unison.

FROM ALL WE CAN LEARN WITH CLOSE INQUIRY, THE WORD RELIABLE MEANS A GREAT DEAL MORE WITH THEM THAN THE ABILITY TO PAY FINANCIAL OBLIGATIONS. THEY ARE SAID TO BE RELIABLE IN INTEGRITY AND EXPERIENCED ABILITY TO ACCOMPLISH WELL THE WORK PROPOSED TO DO.

We [illegible] large building, [illegible] Washington Street, corner of Jay Street, New York. We have made this [illegible] such a chance is seldom offered. The advantages are important: "First, a corner property draws [illegible] Second, the location is much better and a corner shows up goods so much more [illegible] advantages are yours. You naturally seek where you may realize the best results. We have [illegible] of the trade here for [illegible] years, and are known by the principle buyers far and near. We [illegible] place where buyers look for their supplies is a good place to put the goods. We have made this business [illegible] principles. With us you have responsibility, experience and fair dealing. You are [illegible] it will do for you. The old stencil and postal cards can be used as formerly.

Refer to W. D. Barns, Middlehope, and Wallkill Valley Farmers' Association.

Nitrate of Soda

Is the Most Stimulating Fertilizer.

The attention of the farmer is called to the value of Nitrate of Soda as a highly stimulating fertilizer for the production of early vegetables or LATE FORAGE CROPS, especially of ensilage crops. Owing to the drowth this year it will be necessery for the farmers to raise large quantities of feed stuff this fall. The application of from 200 to 400 pounds of NITRATE OF SODA per acre, to ensilage, insures the crop.

IT FORCES RAPID GROWTH.

For Literature upon Nitrate of Soda, apply to
John A. Myers, 12 John St., New York City.

Hawkes, Newburgh; recording secretary, A. B. Hurtin, Middletown; vice president at large, Jas. S. Eaton, Walden; executive committee, H. N. Greene, Washingtonville; M. C. Sears, Blooming Grove; R. H. Wood, Goshen; H. E. Williams, Walden.

At Goshen, May 1899, the attendance from all sections of the county was large, and the sessions of great interest. The address of welcome by Rev. Robert Bruce Clark most cordial. The response from Mr. James S. Eaton, of Walden, voicing the good will of the assembled delegates; all lines of the county work indicated a healthy and growing interest. A new departure was made in ordering the publication of the record of the years work and the minutes of the convention, for distribution in the schools of the county. Entertainment of visiting delegates, by the ladies of Goshen, in one of the Halls of the village, was most ample and elaborate.

We have traced the historical record of the Society from 1872, from the Recording Secretary's book, kindly loaned by the efficient Secretary, Mr. A. B. Hurtin, of Middletown; the preceding eleven years the writer was familiar with the life and growth of the organization, and from our records are enabled to place on file much interesting data that otherwise would pass with the forgotten past.

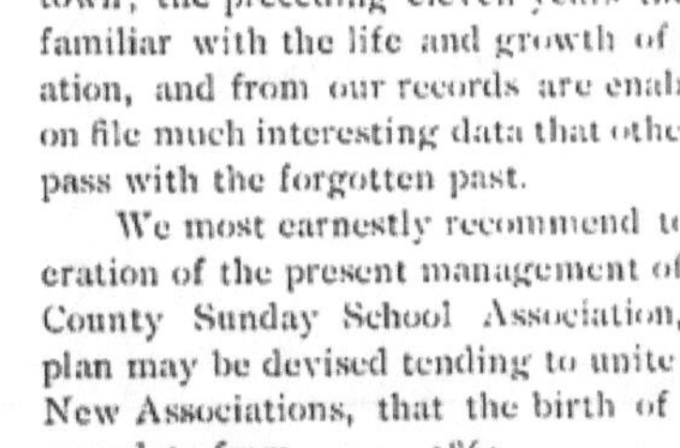

EDGAR C. BARNES.
President of the Orange County Sunday School Association.

We most earnestly recommend to the consideration of the present management of the Orange County Sunday School Association, that some plan may be devised tending to unite the Old and New Associations, that the birth of the Society may date from —— 1861.

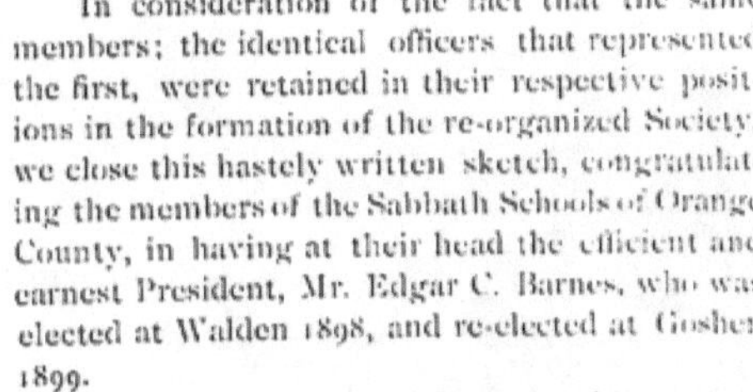

In consideration of the fact that the same members; the identical officers that represented the first, were retained in their respective positions in the formation of the re-organized Society, we close this hastely written sketch, congratulating the members of the Sabbath Schools of Orange County, in having at their head the efficient and earnest President, Mr. Edgar C. Barnes, who was elected at Walden 1898, and re-elected at Goshen 1899.

Mr. Barnes, a native of Orange County, was born July 16th, 1834. His parents removed from the Valley of the Wallkill near Walden, to New York City when he was seven years of age, at which place he received a common school education.

During the cholera epidemic of 1849, his parents returned to Orange County, and at the age of seventeen he entered the employ of A. R. & O. Taylor as clerk in their store at Pine Bush, N. Y. Many of the business principals instilled into him by Archibald R. Taylor during the three years he was there employed have been with him throughout his business life.

Orders Called for and Delivered.

Charles W. Innis & Son,

GROCERS.

202 BROADWAY, NEWBURGH, N. Y.

BUTTER AND EGGS.

Fruits and Vegetables in Season.

Ellen House,

58 Montgomery St., Newburgh, N. Y.

BOARDING

BY THE DAY OR WEEK. MODERN IMPROVEMENTS. FINE RIVER VIEW, WELL VENTILATED AND AIRY ROOMS. ONE BLOCK FROM POST OFFICE.

Front Street Livery Stable,

[illegible] Front St., Cor. Third.

GEO. ELLEN, PROPRIETOR.

Little Fulton Fish Market,

67 FRONT STREET.

TELEPHONE CALL, 115-3.

STANDARD SELF-RETURNING DUMB WAITER.

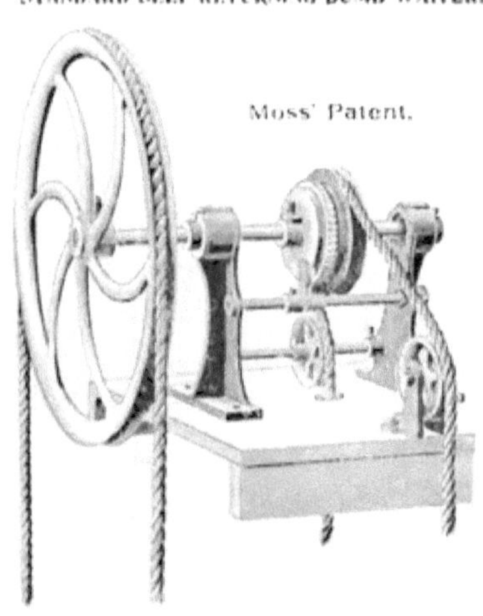

W. G. KIMBALL. ESTABLISHED 1852.

S. G. Kimball's Son

Dealer in Steam Pipes
and Fittings.

Iron and Brass Founder and Machinist

MANUFACTURER OF

The STANDARD
AUTOMATIC
DUMB WAITER.

Repairs of all Kinds and **Jobbing**

OUR SPECIALTIES.

125 to 131 Washington St., Newburgh, N. Y.

ORANGE LAKE, ON THE LINE OF THE ELECTRIC RAILWAY BETWEEN WALDEN AND NEWBURGH.

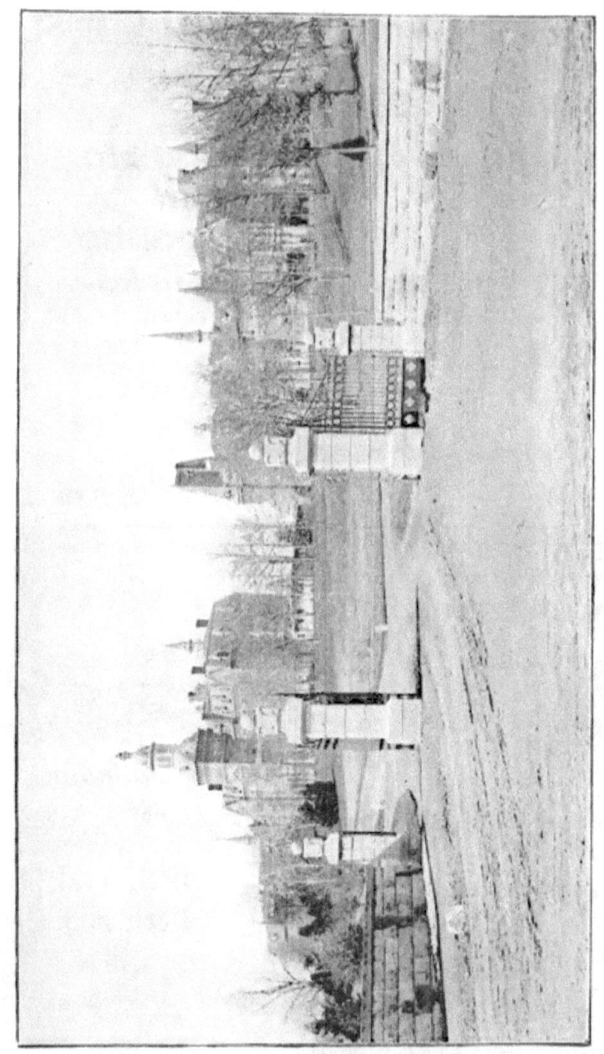

THE MIDDLETOWN STATE HOMEOPATHIC HOSPITAL. SELDEN H. TALCOTT, M. D., MEDICAL SUPT.

David C. Miller,

No. [illegible] Broadway. Newburgh, N. Y.

Granite Monumental
Dealer and Sculptor.

About ten blocks from the River, north side.

FORSON & ROSS

Newburgh, N. Y.

STEAM

Marble and Granite Works.

•••

MONUMENTAL AND CEMETERY WORK FINISHED IN THE BEST POSSIBLE MANNER.

Designs and Estimates Furnished.

GRANITE A SPECIALTY.

GEORGE T. OVERHISER

MONTGOMERY, N. Y.

Funeral Director.

Fine Carriage Painting a Specialty.

Economy in our Prices and the Best Meats the Market Affords.

Charles Johnson,

ST. ANDREWS, N. Y.

DEALER IN

Beef, Veal, Mutton, Pork and Poultry...

My stock is always selected with the greatest care, and is [illegible] with the assurance that for quality it is unexcelled.

VILLAGE AND COUNTRY HOMES REGULARLY SUPPLIED.

WALLKILL VALLEY CEMETERY.

HENRY SUYDAM, President. DANIEL T. TEARS, Superintendent.

ORANGE COUNTY AGRICULTURAL SOCIETY.

Fifty-Ninth Annual

FAIR

Middletown N. Y.

September 12th, 13th, 14th, and 15th, 1899.

For Cattle, Horses, Sheep, Swine, Poultry, Dogs, Implements, Machines, Furniture, Grain, Vegetables, Flowers, Fruit, Bread, Cake, Canned Fruit, etc., Paintings, Drawings, Decorative Works, Fancy Articles, Needlework — plain and ornamental; Domestic Manufactures, School Work, etc. A number of valuable Special Premiums are also offered.

Premiums

AMOUNTING TO NEARLY

$7,000

ARE OFFERED.

An Address by

Governor Roosevelt

on the First Day Tuesday, Sept. 12th.

Trotting Races during the Second and Third Days for purses amounting to $[illegible].

Children's Day, Friday, Sept. 15th when Children attending school will be admitted FREE.

A Grand Cavalcade of Horses each day [illegible] Fair, and other Special Attractions may [illegible]pected.

Excursion Rates on all Railroads. Exhibits returned Free. Electric Cars Run to the grounds.

Entries of Live Stock, including Poultry, close Sept. [illegible]th. Entries in all other classes close Sept. [illegible]th.

Premium Lists

and regulations, with entry blanks, furnished on application to either of the following officers:

Hon. Augustus Dennitson, Washingtonville, President; Benjamin C. Sears, Blooming Grove, E. A. Brown, Middletown, Vice-Presidents; D. A. Morrison, Newburgh, Secretary; William Eager, Montgomery, William F. Royce, Middletown, Assistant Secretaries; H. M. Howell, Middletown, Treasurer.

DIRECTORS:

William H. Hallock, Washingtonville; George A. Swayze, Middletown; William H. Clark, Westtown; V. Edgar Hill, Stony Ford; J. Edward Wells, Chester; Henry M. Howell, Middletown; Sidney H. Sanford, Warwick; Horace D. Thompson, Middletown; S. D. Roberson, Bullville; C. W. Shaw, Mountainville; W. S. Laurence, Chester; Charles Mapes, Middletown.

ADMISSION Member's or Exhibitor's Ticket, $1; Single Admission Ticket, 35c.; Carriage Tickets, 35c.

"MARY, A DAUGHTER OF THE WALLKILL VALLEY."

IF YOU LOVE

Good Horses

BUY A

DEERING MOWER

AND A

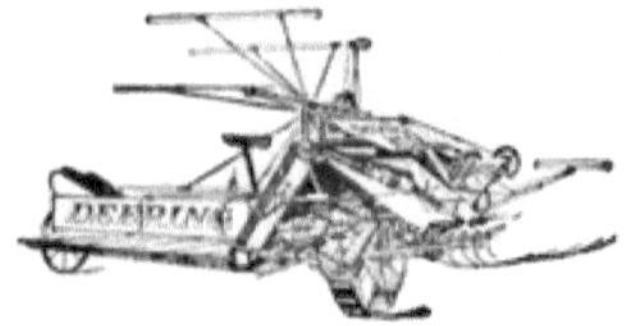

........Deering Pony Binder

To do your mowing and harvest your grain, and you will save them a great deal of labor. Acknowledged to be the lightest draft and best cutting harvesting machinery on the market. Call and examine them for yourselves before buying elsewhere. Every MACHINE FULLY WARRANTED.

FOR SALE BY

Joseph M. Shafer,

WALDEN, N. Y.

Theodore D. Barker,

WALDEN, N. Y.

Harness Maker and Carriage Trimmer.

BUSINESS ESTABLISHED IN 1856.

Harness of all Kinds and a General Line of Horse-Furnishing Goods, a Fine Line of Gloves for all Purposes. Quality and Price Reasonable.

...Horses Bought and Sold...

Main Street,
WALDEN, N. Y.

ONE OF THE ISLANDS OF THE WALLKILL, ORANGE COUNTY, N. Y.

Walden Steam Laundry,

BESSLEY FREAR, Prop.

OAK STREET, WALDEN, N. Y.

☙ ☙ ☙

As Good Work As Is To Be Had Anywhere.

Sustain Home Industry!

Patronize People Who Live and Spend Their Money With You.

Local Agency at John Cox, Montgomery; John White, Wallkill; J. N. Crist, Pine Bush. Laundry Collected and Delivered Free of Charge.

Casper Kniffin,

WEST SIDE MARKET, WALDEN, N. Y.

Dealer in Choice Dressed Steer Beef, Mutton, Pork, Veal and Lamb. Poultry in its season. Kettle Rendered Lard of the Finest Quality. I exercise great care in the selection and purchase of my meats. Our patrons can rest assured that it will be my highest ambition to furnish at all seasons the best the market affords, and on the most liberal terms. Meats delivered. We ask the people of Walden and surrounding country one favor: "As we journey through life let us live by the way."

The Walden Citizen and The Wallkill Enterprise

ISSUED EVERY FRIDAY.

WHITFIELD GIBBS, Editor and Publisher.

All Forms of Job Printing!

OFFICE, MAIN STREET, WALDEN, N. Y.

THE THREE (ELMS) SISTERS. PLAINS ROAD, ULSTER CO., N. Y.

A TYPICAL WHEAT FIELD.

Courtesy of Prof. Roberts, Director of Agriculture, Cornell University.

W. J.

CAMPBELL

ST. ANDREWS, N. Y.

Best Goods

Lowest

Prices

FLOUR

...Patent Process Only...

FISH

....Sweet, Fat, White....

TEAS

Young Hyson, Oolong, Japan, English Breakfast, Gunpowder..........

COFFEES

Java, Maracaibo, Mocha.

Delaware County Butter a Specialty.

CANNED GOODS

Goods Delivered and Orders Solicited.

Do You
Realize ?

That the Heat WASTED IN YOUR CHIMNEY from Stoves, Ranges, or Furnaces, WOULD KEEP YOUR UP - STAIRS ROOMS WARM ALL WINTER ? ☙ The Ross Radiator SAVES THIS HEAT and SAVES ITS COST IN FUEL. ☙ If your dealer don't keep the ROSS RADIATOR WRITE FOR FULL PARTICULARS AND PRICES.

Ross Radiator Co.,

Newburgh, N. Y.

Guaranteed Satisfactory or Your Money back.

☙ Electric Light Plants, Burglar Alarm Systems, House Call-Bell Systems, and Telephone Systems installed, and the best of results guaranteed. ☙ Manufacturers of Special Reactance Governing Board for Series Alternating Current Circuits. ☙ General Sales Agents for Packard Lamps and Transformers. ☙☙☙ When in need of anything in the ELECTRIC LINE, Write to or Call on ☙☙☙☙☙☙☙☙☙☙

Hewitt & Warden,

14 S. Water St.,
Newburgh, N. Y.

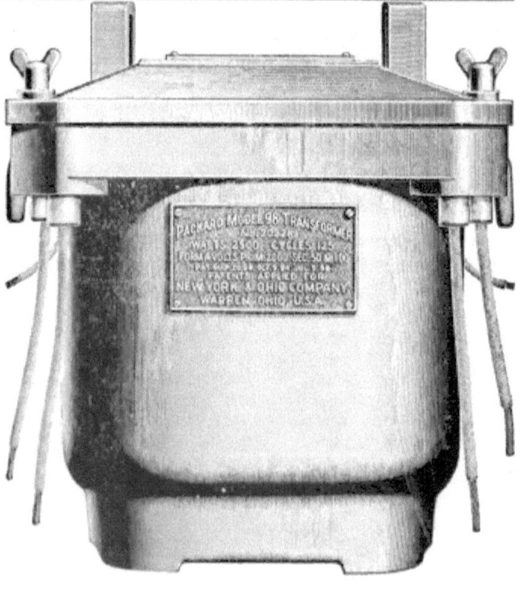

F. W. Devoe & Co.'s

Pure Lead and Zinc Paints.

READY FOR USE!

The Dark Colors, many of which are used for trimming purposes, are solid colors made from the most permanent pigments, and therefore do not contain either lead or zinc.

None of these paints contain any Water, Alkalis, Benzine, Petroleum, Kerosene, Fish Oil, Barytes, Whiting, or other adulterants. They are not "Patent," "Chemical," or "Fireproof."

.They are all Made with Pure Linseed Oil Only.

They are strictly pure and FREE FROM ALL FORMS OF ADULTERATION. They are sold subject to Chemical Analysis. The Whites and Light colors contain only: Pure White Lead, Pure White Zinc, Pure Linseed Oil, Pure Turpentine Dryer, Pure Tinting Colors. THE PAINTS ARE MADE FOR PAINTING HOUSES.

NOTE ALSO—These paints are all put up full measure according to the United States Standard Gallon of 231 cubic inches.

Manufactured by F. W. Devoe & Co., New York, the Oldest and Largest Paint Concern in the United States.

ESTABLISHED 1754.

FOR SALE BY FOWLER HARDWARE CO., WALDEN, N. Y.

Fowler Hardware Co.,

WALDEN, N. Y.

Real Estate and Insurance.

We Make a Specialty of Renting and Selling Village and Farm Property in this Section.

.....The New York Furniture Company...

THE LARGEST HOUSE FURNISHERS IN ORANGE COUNTY.

House furnishers come and go, but the Old Reliable New York Furniture Co. can always be found at

No. 102 Water St., Newburgh, N. Y.

With Reliable Goods at the Most Popular Prices.

Furniture, Carpets and Crockery

In fact, everything to furnish your homes. Here you will find an assortment of goods not found in any other house in Newburgh. If Middletown is more convenient, we carry the same stock at the same prices, at

C. EMMET CRAWFORD'S

44 and 46 North St., Middletown, N. Y.

DAY LINE STEAMER "NEW YORK," PASSING U. S. CRUISER "NEW YORK

ON THE DAY LINE. THE PARK AT KINGSTON POINT.

"In the Shade of the Willows."

PARLOR AND OFFICE OF DR. F. W. SEWARD.

A PRETTY SPOT AT PINE HILL, N. Y.

Alex. Goldberg

Newburgh's Leading Clothier,

Hatter and Furnisher
For Man, Boy or Child.

83-85 Water Street, NEWBURGH, N. Y.

NOISY ALARM CLOCK, **63c**

...Nickel Watch 98c

Leave your Good Watch Home while Fishing, Bicycling, and Working the Farm. Every One WARRANTED.

R. H. GORRIE, Jeweler, 79 Water St., cor. Third St.

NEWBURGH, N. Y.

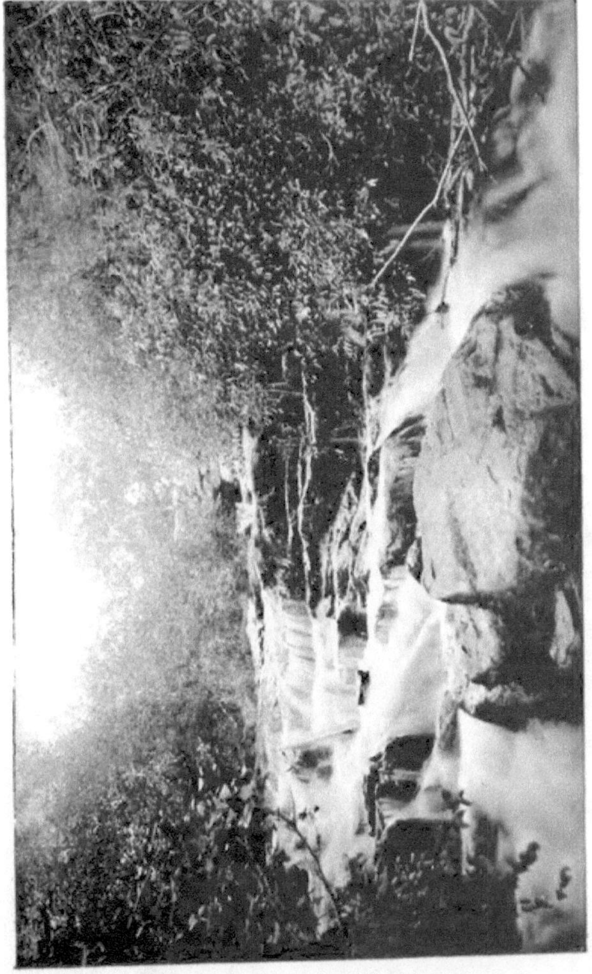

A MOUNTAIN STREAM, NEAR LAKE MOHONK, ULSTER COUNTY, N. Y.

Just one word

and that word is reliability. It is the foundation of success.

Our remedies ARE reliable. Twenty years of increasing demand is the BEST recommend we have.

Scott's Arabian Paste,

The best all-around veterinary remedy known. . . . . . .

25c, 50c and $1.00.

Scott's Gall Paste,

Cures and work the horse every day. . . . . .

25c.

We guarantee our goods if directions are followed. NO CURE NO PAY. Send for price list to the trade. Single boxes on receipt of price.

ARABIAN PASTE is a positive cure for caked udder. Preventative better than cure. One application at the first appearance of inflammation will save the udder. Keep it in the stable. Do not lose the use of a valuable cow by unnecessary delay. Always have a reliable remedy on hand when needed.

SCOTT'S FAMILY PASTE is unequaled as a general household remedy—cures cuts, bruises, burns, scalds, corns, chafing, abcesses, boils, pimples, salt rheum, eczema, cold sores, chapped hands, sore nipples, inflamed breasts, old sores, etc. Sure cure for piles. For bicycle bumps and bruises, there is nothing that will remove soreness and inflammation as quickly. Ask your druggist or dealer for it. If they have not got it they will send for it.

Insist on having the genuine. Take no other. Do not take something that you are told is as good as SCOTT'S, for there are no remedies made that equal Scott's.

SCOTT HOOF PASTE CO., Rochester, N. Y.

CATHEDRAL GORGE—ESOPUS CREEK, NEAR BROWN'S STATION

EDWIN KNAPP

COLDENHAM, N. Y.

CARRIAGE WORKS. Blacksmithing and Repairing. Carriage Painting a Specialty, using only the Best Materials, combined with a thorough knowledge of the work.

Thankful for past patronage of citizens of Wallkill Valley, I invite a continuance of the same, and will give attention to all who may address or call upon me at my business stand.

J. D. MABIE

DEALER IN

STOVES, HEATERS,
RANGES, ETC.

Plumbing, Tinning, Etc.

46 WATER ST., NEWBURGH, N. Y.

JOHN SCHWARTZ
& SONS MANUFACTURERS OF

Fine Cigars

and WHOLESALE
and RETAIL . . . .

Tobacconists

313 MAIN STREET
POUGHKEEPSIE . .

We carry a large and complete line of everything required by Tobacco users . .

Ask for our New Cigar

"The Wallkill Valley Special"

5 CENT CIGAR

Retail Dealers will consult their interests by calling on us . . . .

JOHN SCHWARTZ
& SONS 313 MAIN STREET
PO'KEEPSIE, N. Y.

HARVESTING WHEAT IN CALIFORNIA—A COMBINED HARVESTER, HORSE POWER.

The Cutting Apparatus extends to the right, and excepting the top of the Reel is hidden by the team. The grain heads are conveyed to the Thresher on a moving "Draper," or Apron, similar to that used in the ordinary Binder. Weight, 12,000 pounds; width of cut, 18 to 24 feet; crew, 4 to 5 men; team, 26 to 32 horses; cuts, threshes, cleans and bags 25 to 45 acres per day. A season's run from 3,000 to 3,900 acres. No rain falls during Harvest season.

These machines are made only by California manufacturers and in that State. The plate for this interesting illustration is loaned us; and the accompanying data is given us through the courtesy of

ADRIANCE, PLATT & CO., POUGHKEEPSIE, N. Y.

Manufacturers of the Adriance Buckeye Mowers, Binders and Reapers.

See their advertisement on the opposite page.

ADRIANCE  BUCKEYE

MOWERS, BINDERS, REAPERS, HARROWS.

You have known the Adriance Buckeye Goods a long time and have always known them Favorably.

They are Now Better Than Ever Before

Modern Machines embodying the Best of the original, every later feature that is good, new features of Great Value to the Farmer and peculiar to the Adriance Buckeye.

Because they are the Best they are used on such Model Farms as the Borden Home Farm, the Arden Dairy Farm and by the Best Farmers in the Wallkill Valley and elsewhere.

MANUFACTURED BY

Adriance, Platt & Co., Poughkeepsie, N. Y.

SEND FOR A CATALOGUE.

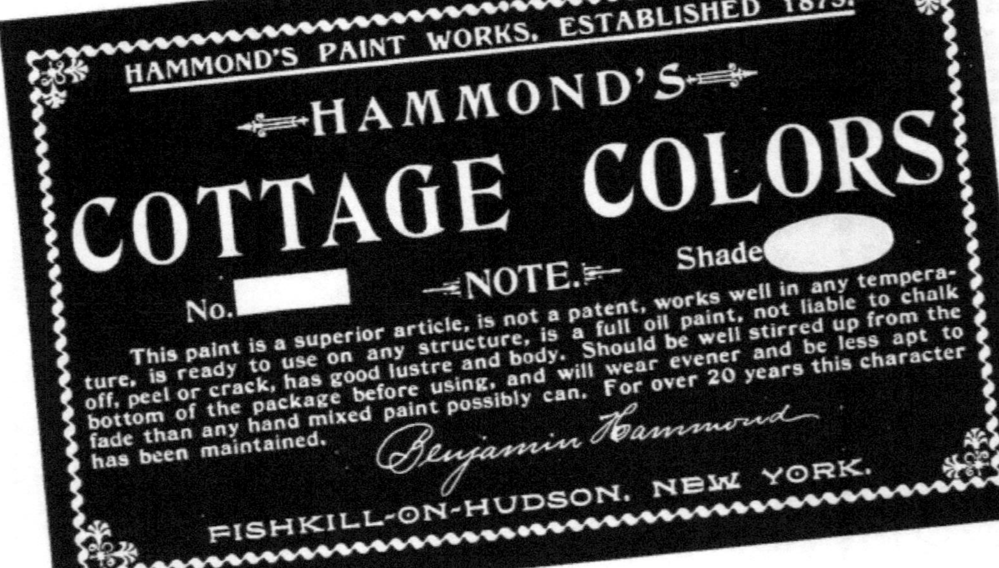

Slug Shot Kills Cabbage Worms

HAMMOND'S SLUG-SHOT 1880 1897 INSECTICIDE & FUNGICIDE

Cattle Comfort

Keep Cattle Comfortable in Fly Time.

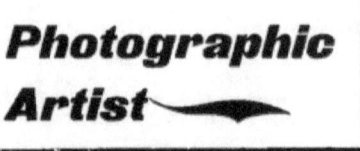

JOSEPH H. ROSE, Pres't.
P. B. SAVAGE, Vice-Pres't.
R. C. WHITEHILL, Sec.
JOHN B. ROSE, Treas. & Gen. Man.
E. W. CORWIN, Ass't Gen. Man.
H. R. P. Co.'s Celebrated
Plumbago Roof and
Stack Paint.
THE HUDSON RIVER PAINT CO.
MANUFACTURERS OF
PAINTS, DRY AND IN OIL.
NEWBURGH, N. Y.
Manufacturers of
all kinds of . .
PAINTS IN OILS .. ..
GREASES, VARNISHES
ETC. . . . .
Plumbago Roof Paints
are the Best . . . . . .
If your dealer does not keep our goods
in stock, write us for samples, prices.

Eagle Hotel

WALDEN, N. Y.

C. JOHNSON.

COMMERCIAL MEN'S HEADQUARTERS.

First-Class Accommodations for Permanent or Transient Guests. This house has recently been refitted and refurnished. Large, airy rooms, electric lights, steam heat, and improved sanitary conveniences. Electric cars pass the door. **Free 'Bus to and from W. V. R. R. Depot.**

TABLE UNEXCELLED. LIVERY ATTACHED.

Main and Walnut Sts., Walden, N. Y.

Nelson House

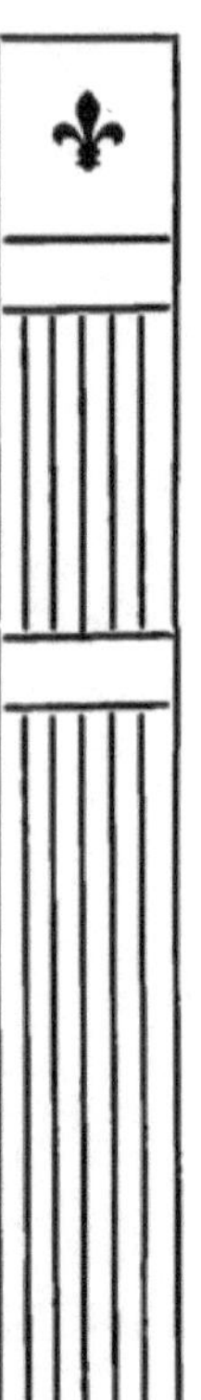

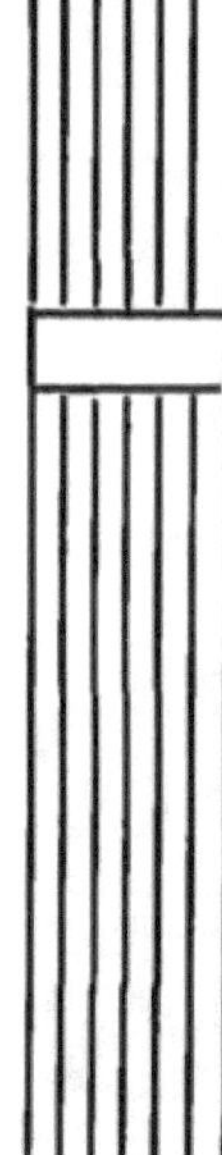

LARGEST AND BEST EQUIPPED HOTEL in THE CITY : : : : :

MARKET STREET
POUGHKEEPSIE::
NEW YORK : : : : :

H. N. BAIN
Proprietor

The Palatine Hotel

NEWBURGH, N. Y.

H. N. BAIN & CO., Proprietors.

MODERN IN CONSTRUCTION AND UP-TO-DATE IN EVERY DETAIL.

The Model Hotel of the Hudson River

The Summer Vacationist makes a mistake if he fails to place this popular Hostelry upon his itinerary

Many Popular Trips out of New York and other places make this hotel their objective point.

The Historical Points of world-wide interest rounding **THE PALATINE** make it popular among tourists.

OFFICERS OF THE

Wallkill Valley Farmers' Association

1899

JOSEPH B. HADDEN
President

HARVEY N. SMITH
Vice-President

WILLIAM C. HART
Secretary

NICHOLAS J. FOWLER
Treasurer

DIRECTORS

Term	Directors
One Year, 1899	JOSEPH B. HADDEN, Walden. GEORGE B. ANDREWS, Walden. WILLIAM C. HART, Walden. JOHN D. MOULD, Montgomery JOHN P. COVERT, Montgomery. ADAM WILEY, Wallkill. LEWIS WOOLSEY, New Paltz. W. H. HALLOCK, Washingtonville.
Two Years 1899-1900	WILLIAM DUNN, St. Andrew's. EDWIN KNAPP, Coldenham. ISAIAH W. DECKER, Walden. ARTHUR McKINNEY, Walden. CHARLES D. WAIT, Montgomery. JESSE BOOTH, Campbell Hall. C. E. STICKNEY, Deckertown, N. J. WILLIAM F. DUBOIS, New Paltz.
Three Years 1898-1901	HORACE D. THOMPSON, Goshen. JONAS DUBOIS, Walden. WILLIAM C. WELLER, Walden. CYRUS W. BOWNE, Walden. HARVEY N. SMITH, Montgomery. ROBERT B. CROWELL, Wallkill. S. HARTSHORN, Plattekill. SAMUEL H. KNAPP, Walden.

Scott's
Emulsion
Cod-Liver Oil
WHAT IS
SCOTT'S EMULSION?
It is a strengthening food and tonic, remarkable in its flesh-forming properties. It contains Cod-Liver Oil emulsified or partially digested, combined with the well-known and highly prized Hypophosphites of Lime and Soda, so that their potency is materially increased.
What Will It Do?
It will arrest loss of flesh and restore to a normal condition the infant, the child and the adult. It will enrich the blood of the anemic; will stop the cough, heal the irritation of the throat and lungs, and cure incipient consumption. We make this statement because the experience of twenty-five years has proven it in tens of thousands of cases.
Be sure you get SCOTT'S Emulsion.
50c. and $1.00, all druggists.
SCOTT & BOWNE, Chemists, New York.

1362